Why is there so much bipartisan bickering?

Why are some folks so darned adamant about their political viewpoints?

Should we all actually develop a political belief system?

But who really gives a hoot about politics, anyways?

Have the schools of this USofA adequately prepared our 18 year olds for one of the important privileges that they can now engage, namely to vote? And even after 18 years old, how and when does each of us actually become EXPERT at selecting our politicians?

How can any one person know who to vote for, and does it really make any difference which way we vote?

They say that if I don't vote then I have no right to complain about who we get in our government. But that doesn't make any sense, or is it just me?

Some say that the MEDIA is biased, but how can that be? They just report the news, don't they?

Why won't our government just do more to FIX things and to HELP people?

What SHOULD our government REALLY do to help us solve our problems?

I've even heard people talk about dark and strange conspiracy theories; about people who are so super rich and powerful, who plan things in secret, and that THEY are the REAL people in control in this world, playing us as if we're all just tokens on a game board...

About the Author

Paul from White Lake is one of the middle children from a family of six. His parents remained married until his Father's death at far too young an age. His Dad was an engineer at a large corporation while his Mom was a stay-at-home Mom. They lived in a far suburb of what had once been one of the top ten cities in the country. Paul is a baby boomer, he went to public K-12 schools, and he worked himself through one of the local State universities, achieving a BS.

Paul considers himself a regular guy, a regular Midwestern corn-fed hard-working American man. He believes that '*integrity*' is one of the most important things in life, and he conducts himself accordingly. He also forever revisits the memories of a speech given by his middle school principal, David Freeman. The speech revolved around the word '*respect*'; respect for your school, respect for your community, and respect for yourself. The '*respect*' concept along with '*integrity*' have remained the main ingredients in everything he's done.

Paul from White Lake wants only to help to fix the country that he's loved his entire life.

What Every 18 yr. Old Needs To Know

A primer for the political novice

by
Paul from White Lake

authorHOUSE®

AuthorHouse™
1663 Liberty Drive, Suite 200
Bloomington, IN 47403
www.authorhouse.com
Phone: 1-800-839-8640

First published by AuthorHouse 2/3/2009

ISBN: 978-1-4389-1034-5 (sc)

Printed in the United States of America
Bloomington, Indiana

This book is printed on acid-free paper.

Table of Contents

I thank my family for all of the squirming that they endured as I gave them little choice but to engage in discomforting discussions of politics.

And especially my sister, Mary, who was willing to dive into the real nitty-gritty of it all and actually get her hands dirty as we focused our thoughts between the two of us.

And most of all, thanks to the wisdom of our Founding Fathers and the Rulebook that they supplied.

God Bless America!

Introduction

When I was growing up there were a few topics that a person wasn't supposed to discuss with others. The reason for avoiding those subjects was because you didn't want to upset another person, or hurt someone else's feelings. A person was supposed to be polite, and in *'polite society'* one simply didn't bring certain things up.

Of course *'politics'* was one of those subjects.

But in a way I was confused by that *'rule'*. I didn't really know anything *about* politics. And how could I ever learn about the subject if I wasn't allowed to discuss it?

So it remained somewhat taboo for many of my formative years.

Somewhere along the way I noticed that *'political'* things *were* being discussed on some news programs on TV. I learned that everyone did *not* think that talking about it was unacceptable; that *some* people *did* talk about it and that talking about it was *not necessarily* improper behavior. But what *really* started to surprise me was that many of the political stories that were being discussed could hardly fall into the category of *'you don't want to hurt someone else's feelings'* much less being *about* people who were participating in *'polite society'*.

My political education began with an occasional quote or speech that I might hear from a politician or a TV news reporter, or an anti-Vietnam war *'demonstration'* that was broadcast on TV news. These *'demonstrators'* and the opposing college campus police were certainly not behaving *'politely'*.

Then I was coming of age. The Vietnam military draft *'lottery'* had been conducted and my birthday had been selected. I was *next up* to be shipped off to the nightmare known as Vietnam.

I asked my Mom about who I should vote for in the next, my first, election. She seemed somewhat befuddled by my question, not quite able to give me the one-sentence guidance a teenager prefers, pontificating on the importance of *'free speech'* but that since we were in the middle of a war, well, if I really didn't know who to vote for then to just vote for the Republican.

Hmm. That really wasn't much help. Besides what I heard on TV news, the only *other* thing I knew about politics was that my folks had always teased each other about canceling out each other's votes. Apparently even my folks didn't see eye to eye.

A sick feeling permeated my gut as I fretted over being sent to war.

1

I suddenly wanted to feel '*safe*', Mom had always needed life to be '*safe*', so maybe she thought that voting '*Republican*' was '*safe*'?

Then I considered all the other kids my age who were also in this same predicament, about to engage in this '*oh-so-important*' activity, namely voting. Did they have any better idea than I had about what to do? I had, after all, run for Student Congress in tenth grade in high school, I had given a campaign speech in front of the entire school, and I had even *won* the election, but I still had no idea of how to proceed in the '*real*' world. I could hear, in my head, the parents of all the other kids giving their own advice. "*Your Father and I have always voted Democrat*", or like my Mom, "*Just play it safe and vote Republican*". I thus resigned myself to believe that I was supposed to '*pick a political party*' and just stick with it, or that for the sake of the '*family*' I was supposed to vote as my parents had always voted as if maybe one's party preference was somehow genetic and was passed on from generation to generation, like hair color, in my genes... But if this were the case, that were I to base my understanding of political issues on the disagreements between my parents then that would only cement my inability to *ever* understand.

The years passed, many elections passed, and always I was there to cast my votes. After all, that's what a good American did. However, entering that voting booth I still had no idea about who to vote for and even *less* of an idea of how my vote was affecting my life and my future. If while reading down the list of candidates there appeared a name that I had seen on a yard sign then I'd vote for *that* person. Other times I might not recognize *any* of the names, but one sounded Irish, so out of respect for my Dad's folks the vote was cast for *that* person. And every time I did these things there would mount a queasy feeling inside my gut, wondering again if anyone else made their voting decisions like I was making mine.

Eventually I embarked on a multi-decade campaign to figure all this political stuff out. I was so disgusted with the audacity of some of our elected officials and with the special '*perks*' they were giving themselves. I was insulted by so many of the arrogant comments I heard them say, acting as if they were superior, a privileged few, and that the rest of us were unimportant peons when all my life I had been taught that we were all created equal. And I was heart broken each time I saw on my pay stub the amount of money that they were taking from me before I'd even had a chance to hold it in my hands. I became determined to find out why *they* thought that *they* should be allowed to continue to *act as they did* and to *do what they did*.

I listened to every political news report that I could. I listened to every radio talk show that discussed political issues. I subscribed to numerous magazines of a political bent, I read numerous numbers of books, I attended political rallies, and I even discussed politics with other individuals who were *not too polite* to discuss these issues.

The more I learned the more disgusted I became. But I tried real hard to keep my cool, to not become a fanatic, to stay level headed when I spoke of all the things that I'd learned, and to not chase others away with the strength of my convictions. Along the way I developed very clear thoughts on so many political topics and I scrutinized my ideas to make sure that my thinking was non-contradictory and logical. I also worked inside my head to learn how to communicate in a simple manner what seemed like very complex political issues.

Then along the way I also noticed that one specific nephew of mine, who happens to be a real level headed brainiac, had been listening to me. His parents divorced while he was still in grade school. He had older half brothers and sisters who were of a strong liberal bent, and he often came to me asking how to respond to them and their liberal arguments. It was *then* that I realized that he was picking up on my own views, my own beliefs, and that somehow I had '*indoctrinated*' him on several things to my points of view. I contemplated that one favor that I could do for him was to help him develop strength in *his own* political beliefs, so I did my best to patiently explain both sides of the issues that he'd ask me about, and then I'd carefully explain why I thought the things I thought.

As the years passed and I studied so many political topics, I discovered that most people really don't care about most things going on in politics. I heard so many just mouthing sound bites that they'd heard from a news reporter, or from a magazine article, and that if you really tried to discuss the topic a little deeper than '*sound bite*' that most were unable to do so. I discovered that so many people really did not have a solid philosophy that helped them define the things that they '*thought*'. However, of those folks who *did* have strong and thorough thoughts on a political issue, it was very often *only one* political issue that they cared about. These folks were '*single issue*' voters. There was only *one* issue that would sway their vote from one candidate to another. I understood their passion, realized that there were a lot more than '*one issue*' out there, but I also saw the value in picking one issue and fighting for the candidates that agreed with their own position.

But then I *also* realized that I had accomplished something rather astounding. I had come to understand *why* so many people vote the way they vote. I could also see so many issues that needed to be fixed when it came to our government, how overwhelming the whole political process was, how difficult it was to keep up with all of the political news going on out there, and how difficult it was for any one person at election time to get their hands around all of the options that they would have to vote for. My heart ached that we as adults would be dumping this whole mess on the next generation of Americans without having sufficiently prepared them (as I had been so ill prepared), and I saw the cleanup/fix up tasks as unfathomable monstrosities. Consequently it seemed that one of the best things that I could do was to help *others* learn more efficiently what it had taken me decades to learn.

And thus this book.

Explaining politics can be dry and consuming. Reading the explanations can be boring and exhausting. While I fear that some of you may find the following discussions to sound like a textbook from back in school, making a point and then proving the validity of the point can indeed require numerous words. However, I promise to make these points as efficiently as possible, because I truly want you to *enjoy* our discussions and even more I want you to *learn* what I have to teach. Please, for the sake of our good ole' USofA, give it your best shot.

Also, it seems our country is in desperate need of getting '*fixed*'. I am thus trying something different (for me) and putting every brain cell to work in order to accomplish this book-writing task. I can only wish that every single high school student could be *required* to read and understand what I've included. Then after the high school students, maybe everyone else, as well.

And by the way, there still exists a '*polite society*' and they're the folks that I prefer. However, '*polite*' must be augmented with strength, smarts, backbone, conviction and a diplomatically clever tongue. Then, once we've developed an entire army of these '*polite*' yet clever tongued voters, we can indeed fix this country.

4

Chapter 1

Civilized Society

A talk-radio show was squawking in the background as I worked a remodeling side job. I like filling the air with thought provoking dialogue while working. The mental gymnastics keep me going. In my corner of the world, when there seems no way to affect any of the world's attitude towards *my* way of thinking, at least *listening* to folks discussing mindful issues keeps me focused, motivated, level headed.

I measured for the next piece of slate floor tile when a self-declared '*liberal*' called the talk-radio show, a young-sounding pleasantly calm, mild-mannered male caller. Being after lunch, the talk show host that was on the air was the controversial Rush Limbaugh. Both Rush and the caller kept their cools as their conversation progressed. They both stayed polite. But I, on the other hand, felt my own blood begin a slow simmer.

"C'mon, Rush" I thought to myself. "Tell the guy what *I* am thinking." But in this particular case Rush either ignored me or he didn't even hear me. "Finally! Once and for all! *Tell the guy* so *they all* will know" I mentally pleaded with the radio. But Rush took the conversation into a direction that was far more entertaining than where *my* request and *my* answer would have taken it.

Their discussion began something like this:

"Why do conservatives and liberals never seem able to conduct a civil conversation with each other?" the caller queried. "Why do conservatives hate liberals so much?"

"Do you mean why should conservatives object to constantly being referred to as heartless, sexist, racist, bigot, homophobes?" Rush responded to the caller's question with a question of his own.

"C'mon Rush" I continued to myself inside my own brain. "This is our chance! Spell it out. Let him *and the rest of them* know exactly why. *You must* know the answer, Rush. And it sure goes deeper than just their vile, deceitful and juvenile name calling."

The caller continued to keep his cool, a seemingly rare condition when a liberal enjoins a conservative talk show. And Rush retained his self-control, too. However, the reference to '*name calling*' made by Rush could itself be viewed as '*name calling*' and could thus have produced a hateful response from the caller if this caller had been of a more typical liberal temperament.

But ultimately the conversation went little further. No mind shattering answers were found. However, they *did prove* that it *was possible* to conduct a civil conversation. Just keep the conversation short and shallow, and avoid taking to heart what the other person says, simple as that.

And it also got *me to thinking*, which was perhaps a result better than simply proving that momentary civility was possible.

In my experience, civility between liberals and conservatives seems rare in normal society when political issues are being discussed. I've been on the receiving end of many abusive verbal attacks and that first hand experience has caused me to analyze what had happened.

In my case I believe that my self-confidence in my beliefs is perceived as close-minded arrogance. And perhaps those liberals might be right about that. But as a result I take great care to state my opinions in the kindest and calmest manner possible, choosing my words carefully, trying not to offend in the *way* that I state my opinions because inevitably the *content* of my views will suffice to turn up the conversation's thermostat.

And do you know what? While I listened to the talk-radio show off working alone where there's no one who's going to hear me, what would it hurt if I let off some steam? So many *other* people lose *their* tempers, and they don't even bother to only do it when they have no witnesses. Maybe I should go ahead and try it out and see how it feels…

No. Wait. I won't do it. I'll accomplish *nothing* by losing my cool except maybe risk causing myself a heart attack. I won't end up '*feeling better*' because I've also learned that what makes me '*feel better*' is when I add things up in my brain and things *finally make sense*. So I'll continue on with thinking things through and instead focus on deciphering the most basic events that occur between individuals, and between individuals and government, and consider how these events overlap with '*politics*'.

Of those most basic events there is one in particular that always bubbles to the top inside my own head. Let's launch our discussion from there:

When you take something that doesn't belong to you, that is stealing. And just because the person who is doing the taking is with '*the government*', you know, those folks with the power to completely destroy your life if you don't comply with their demands, it doesn't mean that it's not stealing. It *is* stealing but its legalized theft.

"*Thou shalt not steal.*" That's one of the ten most basic rules that most of us are taught at the youngest age, one of the most basic rules of a civilized society. But we don't need to venture into religious theology and the fact that it is also one of the Ten Commandments to justify this rule. Just try to take something that belongs to someone else while that someone else is watching, and *see what happens*. The most basic lesson about stealing can be learned quite quickly, effectively, efficiently.

So why should so many people think that stealing is okay when the government does it? And how does the government get away with this? The answer is, *because they can*. And because different people have different expectations of their government.

And because there are plenty of those liberals.

A civil society; just imagine; a society where there are no conflicts between any two individuals. How nice would that be? No wars. No arguments. No hurt feelings. But is this possible? Not as long as human beings are human beings. However, it is certainly an honorable goal to strive towards, and the more civil that we can become the better off we all will be.

So to those ends we as human beings see the necessity of instituting governments.

My thoughts begin to revolve around two concepts that are explicably intertwined, namely the *role* of our government and a civil (or civilized) society. The definition of each of these concepts and how they overlap is from where so many of our heated political discussions stem. In order to continue are discussion with all of us lined up in our thoughts, how about we define the '*role of government*' and what we expect of a '*civilized society*' from the two ends of the political spectrum?

In the two tables on the next page I make a few initial comparisons. After reviewing the *first* table please return here.

Are these definitions a bit too simplistic? Perhaps, but they do identify the extremes of the spectrum; and they also provide us with a foundation from where our discussions can proceed.

Note that there are pros and cons for each of these views and those pros and cons are what confuse and confound we who participate in political discussions.

Further analysis of those different views will also uncover pitfalls to each resulting from how human beings actually function and those pitfalls will sabotage our efforts when striving for our utopian civilized society.

Thus the first table is not complete without including a row that identifies the extreme of the sabotaging pitfalls.

	Liberals	Conservatives
Civilized Society:	That all people have what they need, in equal and '*fair*' proportions	That all people respect all others who have earned respect, and no one takes what belongs to others or what hasn't been earned
Role of the Government:	To do '*whatever it takes*' in order to forever redefine and ensure the equality and fairness for all '*the people*'	To ensure that all are provided a safe environment from where each can strive to earn respect and property and to keep what they have earned if they choose to do so
Sabotaging Pitfalls:	In order for the government to perform the task of ensuring equality it must be given the ultimate power of enforcement over '*the people*'. This ultimate power must manifest as a group of individuals who are not '*equal*' with the rest of '*the people*'. In order for *most* people to be equal, those with the power must be kept to a minimum. This creates a group of elites who are '*anointed*' with their power, the '*power elites*'.	Some folks will earn more than others. Some will have more talent. Some will have a stronger self-motivating will. Some talents will earn more '*respect*' and will be considered more valuable. Thus some folks will inevitably *earn more* and thus *end up with far more* than other people. This inequity will cause these more successful folks to be envied, even hated, by those who believe that things should be evenly distributed.

We immediately see some bumps in this road. The *'conservative'* side has some obvious problems because there exists *'liberals'* while the *'liberal'* side has problems within itself:

1. The most basic *'liberal'* view contains an obvious contradiction that proves right off the bat that their premise is flawed, namely that the only way to ensure that *everyone* is equal is only if some *are not* equal.

2. The government (or *'power elites'*) will try to even the score between the haves and have-nots by *giving* to those with less. However, the government has nothing *unless it takes it* from those who have it. Realistically, evening the score between the haves and have-nots means taking from the haves. It won't be long before the haves will resent the taking. They will do whatever they can to stop the thievery, even to the extent of ending their *own* success. A government *can* kill the goose that lays the golden egg.

3. The government (or *'power elites'*) will enjoy their positions at the top. They will be able to scam and skim with impunity, because, after all, who can stop them? *They* possess the power. The rest of the people are under their control. And as they claim to do *'whatever it takes'* for *'the people'* they will most likely change their focus to doing *'whatever it takes'* to *retain their positions* of power, and *using their power* to ensure that they retain it.

4. The government (or *'power elites'*) when doing *'whatever it takes'* will quite likely resort to doing things to *'the people'* that might be considered *'uncivil'* by some of the people. After all, how else do you force people to do things? By doing things *to them* that at least creates discomfort for them. And if the discomfort isn't enough for the desired results? Then increase the pain; and eventually, with enough pain, the desired result will hopefully occur. Note that one person inflicting pain on another in order to coerce his cooperation could certainly border on being considered *'uncivil'* behavior. So our goal of civility can only be achieved through uncivil means? Another contradiction.

Are the above situations inconceivable? No, they are *inevitable*. We are all after all human beings and that's the way we function.

Will everyone in the government become corrupt? Not necessarily. By definition those who are *truly* conservative will not. Review the tables above for the definition of conservative. If conservatives do become corrupt then they *cease to be* conservative.

So what about those liberals? Will they become corrupt? Don't items 2, 3 and 4 from the above list answer that question? However, let's restate those items in a slightly different manner:

If one believes that taking something from someone else is okay then one is condoning thievery and thus condoning corrupt behavior.

If one believes that one must do *'whatever it takes'* to achieve one's goals is there some imaginary line that is drawn that will *not be crossed*? *'Whatever it takes'* implies that there *is no line.*

And with those two simple statements, the essence of the liberal belief system, *you tell me* whether liberals will become corrupt. I personally believe that they are by definition corrupt although they may not actually realize that they are.

Egad! I think I may have just engaged in a close-minded arrogant slam of liberals. But am I justified? Let's continue.

Can conservatives and liberals find *compromises* that will allow for the composition of a civilized society? Not if conservatives remain conservative. The moment they compromise then they are no longer conservatives. Liberals, on the other hand, can compromise all day long because any results that are not conservative will indeed keep things moving into their *'liberal'* direction.

Now *there* is *another* close-minded arrogant slam of liberals. Why do I keep doing this? Where is my head?

Conservatives versus liberals; it's like having clean hands. Once they get dirty, even just a little bit dirty, they are no longer clean.

It's like mixing white paint. Add *any* color to it and it is *no longer white.*

Am I somehow comparing clean hands and pure white to conservatism? Indeed, I am. But we need more explanation.

Every single compromise that moves you away from conservatism, the dirtier your hands, the less white the paint.

Are conservatives a bunch of holier-than-thou better-than-the-rest-of-us goodie-goodie snobs? Well, actually, no. They are human. No human is perfect. However, conservatism is a place where we all could strive to be. Conservatism is a goal just like a *'utopian civilized society'* is a goal. The more people who strive towards conservatism, the more people that are trying to respect others, the more people who refuse to take what they haven't earned and the result will be less provoked or justifiable incivility between individuals and we move towards a more civilized society.

We *could achieve* a civilized society if everyone was conservative. But alas, there also exist liberals.

So if conservatism is a *'goal'* then what about liberalism? It's not got a definition that is quite so eloquent. In fact, it's not really comprised of a cohesive bunch of folks, either. Let me list a few types of people who I cannot envision as falling into the conservative category. Could they be liberals?

1. Work towards perfection? Yah, right. That's way too hard. It takes lots of effort, focus, studies, strenuous work. It's simply not worth it. Besides, I always fail. So I'll probably just fail again.
2. I'm a human being so I have flaws. Thus, it's a *waste of time and energy* to strive for the impossible dream of eliminating my flaws. I might as well just give up trying and just accept myself as I am. I guess being good enough will have to be good enough. In fact, maybe I should be *appreciated for* my flaws. See my flaws? *In your face!*
3. If only I could manipulate others to feel sorry for *my* problems, *and me*, then I could *get them* to *give* me stuff. After all, there are lots of generous suckers out there.
4. If I could get the psychiatric community to diagnose my *'problem'* as a *'medical condition'* then I might be able to get some insurance company to pay me because of my *'disease'*. But I'll have to really play up the symptoms, and I may need to be *'incurable'*, otherwise the money could dry up.
5. If I could get a lawyer to take my case and maybe even engage a *'class action'* suit, then we could get some bleeding heart jury to render a monstrous verdict and I'd be sittin' pretty.
6. It's *not fair* that others have more than me. *I want* those things that *they* have, *too!* Someone should *do* something.
7. Why can't some one *help me*? I'm only one person. I *can't be expected* to do *everything myself!*
8. I'm not getting a fair shake. Others are picking on me. Others are being prejudiced against me. The government should force those people to stop picking on me. In fact, while we're at it, I want *extra* compensation for all they've put me through, for all the pain and suffering of my past, and how about for all the pain and suffering of my *ancestors*, too?
9. Those people who have so much must have cheated someone to get what they've got. We *must get even* with them!

10. I could join a union, piggyback on the hard work and ethics of *others* in the union, I'll get paid what those *other* guys are worth, and I can have my job protected even when I don't pull my own weight.
11. The only *real* problem with lying, cheating or stealing is getting caught.
12. I don't feel worthy. But if I could take up a cause for the good of society then fighting the battle against those greedy selfish capitalists will…, ahh…, well…, at least I'll know that I gave it my best shot!

And that is indeed who I think the liberals are, the folks who *won't strive* to be the best that we can be, who give up, who blame others, who expect some one *else* to do for them what they won't do for themselves; and even worse are those politicians who *cater to* and *exploit* these slackers.

Are there traits in that list that I admire? Are any of them the type of people who I want to strive to emulate? Are they people with whom I want to even associate? Are they people who we as a society should place on a pedestal and throw accolades upon? Should we reward those who have given up trying to provide for their own needs? Absolutely, positively, no!

And perhaps an even more important question: is it *possible* to have a civilized society if there are too many of those types of people always nipping away at the efforts of those who *are* striving to make things better?

This *is* our dilemma.

How can we reach our civilized society? Is there anything that can be done to achieve utopia when the two sides are so far apart? When any compromise will move us further from one goal and deeper into an inevitable contradictory oxymoronic corruption-inducing predicament? Is one side of our spectrum right and the other side wrong? Is it possible for two such divergent opposing ends of the spectrum to coexist? Or are we simply doomed to ever-enduring never-ending conflicts?

But wait; we're searching for that utopian civilized society, aren't we? Solving this problem should be worth the effort, no? So *how do we* solve this problem? In fact, how do we solve *any* of society's problems?

One thing we *could* do is to '*just react*'. And there are probably lots of folks who would do just that. However, maybe before we '*just react*' we might first take a deep breath and count to ten.

One, two, three, four… Hey, wait! I think I have an idea…

12

The *civilized* way to solve a problem might be to start by *thinking it through*.

But does this *feel* right?

I'm not sure. In fact, I'm not sure *what* I feel about this…

It would sure be a lot easier to *'just react'*. But would that really result in a *real* solution that would *really* work? Maybe; maybe not. But you know, I *was* given a brain. Maybe I should *try* to use it? But that means *'thinking'*, and *'thinking'* is *hard*. Wouldn't it be easier to just..?..?..?..

Hey, wait. This is for *all of mankind*, for a *utopian civilized society*; maybe it *is* worth the extra effort.

So we're back to *'thinking it through'*…

And how do we do that? Well, let's think…

Two things are required.

First, we need the facts, scientific, cold hard facts. Second, we need to logically analyze the facts, logically assemble the facts, and logically arrive at a logical conclusion. It's really that simple, facts and logic.

But the facts must be *real* facts. Not fears, maybes or what ifs. Facts can't be proven wrong; otherwise they aren't facts. Two plus two indeed equals four. If it didn't then it wouldn't be a fact.

And what about the fears, maybes and what ifs? Well, let's see. What side of the bed did you get up on this morning? Are you having a *'good hair day'* today? Tell me, exactly, how do you feel today? Fears, maybes and what ifs fall into the non-fact *'how you feel'* category. They originate from every part of the body while *'thinking'* occurs in only one part. Many of most people's *'how you feel'* experiences originate in what we refer to as the *'heart'*, a most valuable body part. However, it is still not where *'thinking'* takes place. And except for some types of headaches which certainly fall into the *'how you feel'* category, the *'brain'* has an exclusive function as the only place where *'thinking'* occurs.

There *are* very acceptable times and places to discuss your fears, maybes, and what ifs. How about giving your Mother a call and chat for a while? Or what about scheduling yourself an appointment with a therapist? Or maybe you just need to take a long quiet walk?

Sure, feelings are part of the human condition, but they are *not* facts. Indeed enjoy your feelings, explore them, and even exploit them. However, reserve them for your creative expression, for your lovemaking, for interpersonal relationships, and for your relaxation, religious and recreational pursuits. But if you want to *solve a problem* then you *must deal with facts*. For the fears, maybes and what ifs, go ahead and wring your hands. *Just keep them out of* the problem-solving endeavor (if you want a *real* solution that *really* works).

Then comes the logical analysis; this can be viewed as a science although it isn't taught as thoroughly as is math. If one is less than two and two is less than three then one is less than three. Again I've oversimplified. However, *'formal logic'* is an interesting science and in fact it was the most fun and fascinating class I took during my undergrad years.

The more facts that you can accumulate and the more logically that you can think, the better your chances of finding a *real* solution that *really* works.

But what if facts and logic don't make me *feel good*? Well, actually, facts and logic don't really *care* about your feelings and they *have none* of their own. My best advice, again, is to keep the two separate. Utilize facts and logic for thinking, feelings for non-thinking. And ultimately you will discover, like I did, and as I mentioned earlier in this chapter, that when all your thoughts add up and make sense that you too could gain a peaceful feeling inside.

So to recap, we have three options for finding a solution. We could *'just react'*, or we could dwell on *'how we feel'*, or we could use our brains to *'think it through'*. The only *intelligent* method for a functioning and *intelligent* human being is the latter, obviously.

I *also* believe that most human beings if given the facts and if taught to think logically *could participate* in this *'thinking'* experience.

And we are indeed most likely to close in on our utopian civilized society if we use our brains. We are human beings. We all have brains. We all really ought to learn how to use them.

Thinking back to Rush Limbaugh and his caller I realize that the reason that there was civility between the two of them wasn't just because the conversation was short and shallow. It's because neither of them indulged in *'just react'* nor *'how they felt'*. Instead they kept their brains engaged. Indeed civility was achieved only by keeping the discussion at an intellectual level, and with lots of self-control on both of their parts to keep it there.

Now what? Oh yah. We're seeking a civilized society.

We should use our brains. And in doing so we'd recognize the importance of coming up with a bunch of rules for *all* of us to live by. The rules would make sense and be the best rules that we could possibly come up with because we had studied the facts and *'thought it through'* as thoroughly as possible. In fact, if we were really smart we would have assigned this rule-writing task to a bunch of guys that we might call our *'Founding Fathers'*. We would then stick these fellows in a room until they had written those bunches of rules in an orderly fashion, using words that all *'the people'* could understand (assuming they could read English and think somewhat logically). And we could call those rules *'The U.S. Constitution'* or something like that, and the result would be to institute a *'government'* that would represent the people. Finally, we all could read the rules and decide whether the rules were good, or at least good enough for now.

And so that's exactly what we did.

But we still didn't reach our utopian civilized society. And why is that? Is it because conservatives and liberals can't get along? Well, that's part of it but it's *also* because some people think and some people don't.

Conservative versus liberal; some folks will slide effortlessly into one of these categories. However, some can't nor do they *want to be* categorized into *either*. Some of them believe themselves to be *'open minded'*, or *'moderate'*, conservative on some issues, liberal on other issues, and unsure on others.

However, my belief is that absent facts and logical thinking a person will tend towards the liberal category and when a person is given all the facts and he logically analyzes and adjudicates those facts he will tend towards the conservative category. For those who are not tending towards conservatism? They need to start thinking a whole lot more.

But how can you think things through without *all* of the facts? And which person can ever *accumulate* all of the facts? Who has the time and energy to perform a thorough logical analysis? With all of the information that comes at us, from different perspectives, and with the information disseminators each having *their own* agendas and each trying to sway our thinking into *his* direction... And how many folks are clear enough thinkers that they can tell when a fact isn't a fact but instead just an opinion? We all have opinions but opinions are not the same as facts, nor are they necessarily even *based* on facts.

And just how many people are clear enough thinkers that they can perform an honest analysis, truly thinking things through, and not allow their emotions to substitute for a functioning brain?

Ultimately, a large number of folks will end up *'unsure'* about many issues. They are the folks who most likely can be swayed in their thinking. And they are some of the people who make our society interesting, exciting, but also vulnerable. Swaying those very folks is what so many on both sides of the political spectrum are trying to accomplish. But swaying them is an arduous task, a never-ending task, after all, the world keeps changing, and there's so little time...

Why are so many *'unsure'*? If it is due to *'not enough time'* then perhaps there is a solution awaiting us just around the corner with the next technological breakthrough. But if it is due to laziness, stubbornness, and/ or ignorance, then our society indeed is vulnerable. The *more people* who are actually participating in our political process who are lazy, stubborn and/or ignorant, the *more vulnerable* we all become because the chance of intelligent solutions being adopted diminish.

Earlier I referred to the '*open minded*' and the '*moderates*'. Neither of these groups is quite as '*safe*' or '*non-descript*' as their names imply. '*Moderates*' believe themselves to be '*middle of the road*'; not extreme in their views into either political direction. However, if they are truly '*half way*' between liberal and conservative then they are no different from the '*compromises*' that we also mentioned earlier. Any '*compromise*' with a liberal *always moves you deeper into the liberal abyss*. Thus '*moderates*' are '*liberals*', too.

Then there are the '*open minded*'. These folks actually fall into one of two different categories. Some are acknowledging that they don't know enough on particular issues but that they are ready and willing to hear the arguments pro and con, to hear the '*facts*' in order to make their choice. Thus this portion of the '*open minded*' group are actually some of the '*unsure*' mentioned above. The balance of the '*open minded*' group *also* acknowledge that they don't know enough but they really won't do any '*thinking*' were they *given the* '*facts*'. Thus they are quite likely to '*just react*' or to respond based on '*how they feel*' and we've already discussed into which political direction the '*non-thinkers*' lean.

So in other words, the '*moderates*' and the '*open minded*' are in reality either '*unsure*' or '*liberal*'.

The world is full of problems. Some get better, some get worse. But always, always, there will be problems.

Can we fix them? Sure we can, but only if we become un-'*unsure*'. We must solve those problems with *real* solutions that *really* work. And for the solutions to work our brains must be utilized to their utmost capacities.

But mustn't we also incorporate our feelings in the decision making process? *Not* if we want a *real* solution that *really* works! Making ourselves feel better is an admirable goal, and a necessity of the human condition, but *emotions must not be used when problem solving*. Go ahead and utilize your feelings to motivate yourself to get out there and help solve problems. But in order to not sabotage your *results*, keep emotions away from your intellectual problem solving.

So where is this fine line where we have suddenly crossed into the *'feelings'* part of our being and out of the *'thinking'* part of our being when it comes to problem solving? For some of us that are inexperienced, recognizing that line can be difficult. Thus consider the following as you develop your ability to locate that line. *It is when the solution that is proposed will make us feel good even though there are facts and honest statistics that show that what will actually occur will not really solve the problem.* And if you have no facts or honest statistics that show what will occur, then find the facts, conduct an honest study, but don't fool yourself into believing that you've solved a problem just because now you feel better.

Many of our problems are thrown into the political arena where they are debated. In come the conservatives, the liberals, and the unsure. It is far too often that we seek our solutions in the political arena. It is said, after all, that we live in a democracy, that all voices are needed as input for us to find the correct solution, and then a *'vote of the people'* for the final decision. But beware. There are *so many fallacies* in that above statement!

All we want is a civilized society. All we need to do is *think* in order to achieve it. Even though the brightest amongst us have written down rules for us to follow in order to achieve our civilized society, we still have not yet achieved it.

And why is that? Because some folks cannot follow the rules (see the next chapter); because of the pitfalls and contradictions in our belief systems; because of the inevitable corruption that some in our government will partake; and while the true complete conservatives' belief system is 100% civil, the liberals' *belief system* is by definition a contradictory oxymoronic corruption-inducing predicament that cannot succeed unless it is *uncivil*.

Chapter 2

Some Don't Like The Rules

Going in we can see that if everyone doesn't cooperate in our attempts to reach for a civilized society then we're in for difficulties. However, the more folks who follow the rules then the better our chances for reaching our goal.

But some folks don't *like* our rules; they don't '*feel good*' about our rules, *especially* when those rules *stop them from doing what they want to do*.

Certainly there will be rules that some won't like. There may be rules that no longer make sense. There may be rules that should never have been written in the first place. So included in our rules *must be* a definition for how to create new rules and how to eliminate those that no longer apply.

And indeed our rules include those definitions. However, our '*Founding Fathers*' purposely made that process laborious in order to try to ensure that the rules written along the way were not flippant seat-of-the-pants immediately gratifying but long-term detrimental.

Some folks don't want to wait out the laborious process; some folks know that the rules *they* desire don't have a rat's chance of getting included into the rulebook; some folks want to keep *their* rules secret so that they can '*get away with*' something without the watchful eyes of others. Let's not be shocked; it's human nature; that's the way that we human beings function. Many among us will look for an edge.

So what will these folks do?

Some will simply ignore certain rules. They'll stay out from under the radar in their efforts to not get caught. They'll hide their shenanigans as best they can for as long as they can. But eventually someone else who knows the rules will find out. Then *that* person will be in the predicament of a few different options. He could look the other way and allow the criminal to continue his crimes. He could request from the criminal a piece of the action in payment for keeping his mouth shut. He could receive from the criminal terrorizing threats, or worse. Or he could throw caution to the wind and report the misdeeds to the authorities.

Eventually after time passes more and more folks will learn of the criminality and someone will indeed come forward and report the crimes. And actually our civilized society *depends* on that eventually occurring;

it depends on there being individuals who understand the necessity of playing by the rules. Otherwise our civilized society is doomed to fail.

It is also crucial to punish those who don't follow the rules not only to end the criminal activity of those criminals but also as a disincentive for others who might consider participating in their own criminal activity.

If too many people get away with criminal activity then we are reduced to living in an uncivilized society. Can anyone think that we are civilized if some folks are allowed to break the rules with impunity?

But then it becomes all that much more important that our rules are the *right* rules, not just rules that are flippant seat-of-the-pants immediately gratifying but long-term detrimental.

Another option for those folks who don't like the rules but don't want to change them as they are supposed to be changed, nor do they want to experience the punishment for getting caught not following the rules, is to carefully connive, to be cleverly devious, and to set out to do '*whatever it takes*' to *manipulate* the *words* in our rulebook to mean something that they were *never intended* to mean.

How might someone go about doing this? Let's count the ways:

1. Convince 'the people' that the rules are far *too complicated* and confusing for an ordinary person to understand. *It requires a lawyer to decipher* the code.

   Problem is I have read our basic rulebook and I understand it. And I don't even have a law license.

2. *Install judges who will write their own laws*.

   Now *here* is a topic that *is actually discussed* openly in current political discussions. Perhaps some folks don't quite understand the ramifications of this issue. The U.S. Constitution states:

   "Article. I. Section. 8. The Congress shall have Power…To make all Laws which shall be necessary for carrying into Execution…all…Powers vested by this Constitution in the Government of the United States, or in any Department or Officer thereof."

   In simpler words, the U.S. House of Reps and the U.S. Senate shall make all laws.

   However, for many years there have been judges who '*interpret*' laws the way that they (and the folks on their '*side*') desire. In many cases these interpretations are so far beyond or askew the justifications they site from within U.S. law that many now refer to what these judges are doing as '*legislating from the bench*', or in other words, writing their own laws. Most recently some of these judges are so blatant about disregarding our own '*rulebook*', the U.S. Constitution, that they have stated that they will (ignore what the U.S. Constitution states and instead) look to '*international law*' for their justifications for rendering their decisions.

Outrageous? Absolutely!

3.   <u>*Refer to the U.S. Constitution as a living, breathing document*</u>. *That* will help justify any misinterpretation that the '*cheats*' try to use against us. That statement implies that while the document just sits there it changes, grows, or maybe even mutates through some supernatural metamorphosis. Perhaps it even has feelings.

It *can* in fact be changed *but only* through the amendment process that is clearly defined within the U.S. Constitution, that laborious process referred to above. It *cannot* be changed automatically nor simply on the whim of some government employee.

4.   <u>*Imply that the U.S. Constitution says things that it does not say*</u>.

How many times have I heard our country referred to as a '*democracy*'? Even by leading government officials, even by Presidents of either major political party. The U.S. Constitution states:

> "Article. IV. Section. 4. The United States shall guarantee to every State in this Union a Republican Form of Government"

And even our Pledge of Allegiance states, with our right hand over our hearts:

> "…and to the republic for which it stands…"

In fact, the word '*democracy*' is *never once* used in the entire U.S. Constitution.

So why do our politicians, and our schoolteachers, so often refer to our country as a '*democracy*'? Could it be that they are once again trying to throw us off the scent?

There *is* a governing document that does indeed reference (a form of the word) '*democracy*'. To quote:

"…it will establish a democratic constitution…"
And from exactly which '*governing document*' is this quote taken? *The Communist Manifesto.*

5.   *Keep 'the people' stupid.* Do not supply them the tools that they would need in order to understand what the '*rulebook*' states.

       For instance: never publicize the existence of the "*Federalist Papers*" or the "*Anti-Federalist Papers*", all those letters and articles written by the Founding Fathers at the time of the composing of the U.S. Constitution. Those letters describe and discuss the pros and cons of the ideas either included or excluded from the U.S. Constitution, and the reason for inclusion or exclusion.

       We certainly don't want '*the people*' to do any further investigation and learn how the government is *supposed to* act, do we?

       In fact, the less able '*the people*' are to effectively '*think*' then the more likely they will '*just react*' or make decisions based on '*how they feel*'. This makes those people easier to manipulate. And the less they can '*think*' then the less able they will be to take care of themselves as '*capable adults*'. They will become ever more vulnerable, and not just with regards to the manipulators in our government but to any nefarious individual who is looking for '*a sucker*'. The non-thinking people who become victimized by the unscrupulous eventually become desperate for '*someone to do something*'. Instead of looking to themselves for a solution they look to the government. This cycle repeats itself over and again until it is spiraling out of control.

       Note that some might even envision a government school system where the government uses money supplied by '*the people*' to finance their endeavors to keep '*the people*' stupid and to teach '*the people*' that when there is a problem they should automatically ask '*the government*' to find a solution. Why, this idea could help to self-perpetuate the whole darned mess of '*keeping the people stupid*'. But who on God's earth would fall for a scheme like that?

6.   Find some passage within the U.S. Constitution that can be twisted in its meaning to somehow authorize the U.S.

government to write *any* law about *anything* that they desire. And they found two such passages. Many folks refer to one of them as '*the commerce clause*' *and* the other is "*for the... general Welfare*". You could drive a Mack truck through the two of these. The U.S. Constitution states:

> "Article. I. Section. 8. The Congress shall have Power To...provide for the common Defense and general Welfare...and...To regulate Commerce with foreign Nations and among the several States..."

Especially in today's day and age, it seems that almost anything that goes on could be interpreted as providing for the general welfare or as affecting international or interstate commerce. Heck, a spider biting an accountant in North Dakota who works out of his own kitchen and is contracted to do work for a trucking firm that moves avocados from California to Rhode Island could be viewed as affecting interstate commerce. We must certainly need the U.S. government to write a law concerning the proper fumigation process to be followed in all in-home offices of contract accountants in North Dakota. No?

7. *Write so many laws that no one can possibly read them all* even if he spent his entire lifetime trying to do so. And when writing them, make sure that they are written in legalize, not plain English, and refer to previously written laws, even changing the meaning of previously written laws via the new laws, so that no normal person can possibly make sense of current law.

8. Convince '*the people*' that since these rules were <u>*written by a bunch of rich, racist, white males a very long time ago*</u> they can't possibly be '*fair*' rules nor can they possibly address the types of issues that face us today.

    Problem is I'm not rich nor am I racist and our rulebook seems '*fair*' to me. It also seems to address today's issues if I engage my brain when reading it and thinking about the issues versus the rules.

    However, I *am* a white male. But the pigmentation of the contents of my trousers does not affect the effectiveness of my brain. Those contents may at times make it less desirable to *want* to engage my brain, but that's a very separate non-intellectual matter, one that falls into the '*just react*' and the '*how you feel*' categories.

9. <u>*Ignore certain words*</u> such that in doing so alters the meaning of the phrase that contains them, <u>*or interpret words to mean one thing in one phrase but something* diametrically *different in another phrase*</u>.

     In this case, let's find an example and compare how some people '*interpret*' the example:

     > "Amendment I. Congress shall make no law…abridging the freedom of speech, or of the press, or the right of the people to peaceably assemble…"

     > "Amendment II. A well regulated Militia, being necessary to the security of a free State, the right of the people to keep and bear Arms, shall not be infringed."

     Some folks will say that '*the people*' referred to in the *First* Amendment means everyone, all of us, while '*the people*' referred to in the *Second* Amendment means *representatives of* '*the people*' such as the police, the military, the National Guard, or any number of the alphabet soup agencies in Washington D.C. In other words, those folks say that '*the people*' referred to in the *Second* Amendment means '*the government*' and *not* '*everyone*' or '*all of us*'.

10. <u>*Change the meaning of words in our current language*</u> to mean something different from their historical meaning.

     Another example is called for here. A reference used immediately above really sticks in the craw of some folks. I thus find it especially pleasing to use it in my discussions:

     > "Amendment II. A well regulated Militia…"

     I have so often heard that the phrase above refers to '*the military*' or '*the National Guard*'. Problem is when looking into history a reading of, say, for instance, the Constitution of the State of Michigan, any version of that document *other than* the first version or the most current version, there is an entire section titled "*Militia*". In that section it defines '*militia*' as:

     > "…all able bodied males between the ages of…"

     To me the words "*all able bodied males*" is a far cry from '*only the military*'.

     And while we're at it, let's dwell on this second Amendment topic just a few moments longer.

     a. Why was that "*Militia*" section removed from the most recent version of the Constitution of the State of

Michigan? Could it be that someone wanted the historic meaning of the word '*militia*' to be lost and forgotten so that eventually when noted in the reading of the U.S. Constitution that the word might be misconstrued to have a meaning different than originally intended?

b. I find it fascinating that our Founding Fathers when writing down our rules for a civilized society found it necessary to include a discussion of '*arms*' (or to use more common current lingo, '*guns*'). To many folks, talking about '*guns*' and '*civilized society*' in the same sentence is down right contentious. Indeed if you '*think*' in terms of '*fears*', '*maybes*', and '*what ifs*' then I can see your point. Well actually, no, I *can't* see your point. That's not '*thinking*'. However, if you engage your brain when combining the two phrases '*guns*' and '*civilized society*' in the same discussion they make *a lot of sense*.

c. What about that *first* version of the Constitution of the State of Michigan? It *did* also include that "*Militia*" section. However, it defined '*militia*' as:

> "...all able bodied white males between the ages of..."

Now *that's* a little bit different. Apparently this northern State had racism written right into its Constitution. That racism was removed a long time ago, and I'm glad that it was. I, for one, truly *appreciate* and *need* all my non-white brethren who *engage their brains*. In fact, the more the better.

11. <u>*Call for a Constitutional Convention*</u> so that the entire document can be scrapped and replaced in one fell swoop.

Indeed this may seem to be a long shot. However, that's how our U.S. Constitution was written in the first place. Those Founding Fathers had actually been sent to their room to '*fix*' the *Articles of Confederation* that had been our previous '*rulebook*'. They ended up throwing out those "*Articles*" and composing the U.S. Constitution.

Also, it is far more common for the separate States to call for a Constitutional Convention for replacing their own State Constitutions (as opposed to the U.S. government calling for a rewrite of the U.S. Constitution). For example, in the current Constitution of the State of Michigan it is written:

"... in each 16th year ... the question of general revision of the constitution shall be submitted to the electors of the state. If a majority of electors voting on the question decide in favor of a convention ... delegates ... shall convene..."

In other words, in Michigan, every 16 years a Constitutional Convention is automatically proposed and if the people choose then a Convention will be held.

So beware. This is *not* such a long shot.

Is the above list a complete list? Probably not; there are likely more items that can be added to the list. My problem with composing such a list is that I don't '*think*' like a deceitful government manipulator so my brain doesn't connive like their brains do. Instead, I must sit back and observe; the above list results from what I have observed.

The con artists have themselves numerous ways to get *their* way in a manner that isn't obvious to the typical person. And should anyone *suggest* that any of the above shenanigans are being attempted, the con artists will simply call the accuser a '*lunatic conspiracy theorist*'. In fact, name-calling is a favorite technique used by deviants to respond when their dishonest tactics are exposed and they do so in order to shut the accuser up and to hopefully send the accuser scurrying away with his tail between his legs. After all, how could a '*lunatic conspiracy theorist*' maintain any self-respect now that he's been labeled as some type of social misfit?

Name-calling; it occurs so often. It must certainly be an effective tool for winning a debate. Or is it?

Those people who don't have an intelligent argument participate in name-calling. Those people who name-call are those who have no facts and perform no logical analysis. In other words, they are amongst the people who do *not* '*think*'. They '*just react*'. They aim for their opponents' '*feelings*'. They turn the debate '*uncivil*'.

Do *I* sound like some kind of conspiracy theorist? If you think perhaps yes then consider the following. There is *another* interesting phenomenon that has occurred in political discussions in our current society. Our '*talking heads*' on TV news shows have come up with a name for those unique people who suggest that the U.S. Constitution might be viewed as meaning what it says and what it was actually intended to say. They call these people '*originalists*'. Isn't that nice? A quaint little name. However, I, for one, wouldn't call these '*originalist*' people names. Instead I would describe them as true '*thinking*' Americans who know how to read, who know how to gather up *real* facts, who recognize that words mean things and who know how to *think*.

Unique concept? Perhaps.

Have I, in this book, indulged in name-calling? Indeed I have. And I apologize. It solved no problems. It was uncivil of me to do so. But as long as I do it in the privacy of my own home, just between my laptop computer and me, and I don't aim it at anyone in particular, perhaps it helped me to let off some steam. And it certainly helps to motivate me to keep on trying, to keep on striving.

We seek a civilized society. We need a way to accomplish this goal.

We view this goal as a problem that needs a solution. As human beings we have three ways of addressing a problem: we can *'just react'*, we can respond based on *'how we feel'*, or we can *'think it through'*.

The greatest likelihood for us to find a truly successful solution would be to utilize only the *'thinking'* method.

Using the best political brains available, we composed a set of rules to live by. Then State by State we joined the union of States that agreed to live by these set of rules because State by State we determined that these set of rules was the best thing going.

But some people don't like the rules because those rules tie their hands. So some people ignore those rules while others twist those rules for their own benefit. Let me restate those ways in an easy-to-reference list.

Top Eleven Methods for Twisting the Meaning of Our Rulebook:

1. Too complicated. It requires a lawyer to decipher
2. Install judges who will write their own laws
3. Refer to the U.S. Constitution as a living, breathing document
4. Imply that the U.S. Constitution says things that it does not say
5. Keep 'the people' stupid
6. The commerce clause and for the general welfare
7. Write so many laws that no one can possibly read them all
8. Written by a bunch of rich, racist, white males a very long time ago
9. Ignore certain words or interpret words to mean one thing in one phrase but something different in another phrase
10. Change the meaning of words in our current language
11. Call for a Constitutional Convention

So here we are. We have a set of rules and plenty of ways to avoid following those rules.

The folks who *do* follow our rules are doing their best to support our civilized society.

The folks who *don't* follow our rules are rejecting our ideas for constructing our civilized society. The criminals who simply ignore our rules are engaging in the most uncivilized behavior, namely criminality, in it only for themselves and anyone who gets in their way be-damned. Those folks who get in the way of a criminal indeed become victimized. Other folks will be less directly affected by the criminality but they too are victimized although they likely won't even realize it. The number of victims increase and our civilized society inches further away.

The deviously conniving who try to twist our rules also cross over the line into uncivilized behavior because they participate in changing the intended meaning of our rules which ultimately sabotages those rules. If the meanings are manipulated then folks either can't know what the rules really mean, or they start following the twisted rules that were never composed as part of our rulebook, or they throw up their hands in frustration from not knowing which way is right and instead they do whatever they themselves decide to do. When all the confusion of some living by one set of rules and others living by a twisted set of rules and still others doing whatever they want to do, the incivility amongst and between each group only intensifies. Everyone is following a different set of rules. Our efforts to attain a civilized society are sabotaged. Anarchy abounds. And anarchy is *not* the same as freedom.

Then we have those folks who participate in '*civil unrest*' in order to affect change. If this '*unrest*' amounts to nothing more then lots of noise then chances are that our civilized society will not be jeopardized. This is after all just '*free speech*'. However, if the '*unrest*' extends beyond just noise then civilized behavior is again being breached. Either way, some folks will notice and listen to those voices. Sometimes our government will respond to those voices. Sometimes those voices will be rewarded with some type of '*payoff*' to quiet them. These '*payoff*'s may be in the form of *special rules* written by the government, *money* provided by the government, or *lots of attention* from media organizations, or in other words, '*special treatment*' for the squeaky wheel. Special treatment for some means no special treatment for others. This unequal treatment will cause resentments to intensify and our civilized society will again become ever more blurred, more obscure, and further away.

But the '*solution*' shouldn't be '*special treatment*' for some. If serious analysis is performed with all the facts having been presented, it may be determined that an existing rule may indeed need to be reviewed, changed, or even eliminated for the sake of our civilized society. However, that isn't how our current government usually functions. The solutions *they* implement usually involve *more* restrictions and *more* rules, and those require *more financing* be supplied to the government in order to enforce the additional restrictions. The result is an ever-increasing government that takes more from the '*haves*'. The resentment increases. The incivility increases.

So what about our three categories of people discussed in the previous Chapter: '*conservatives*', '*liberals*' and the '*unsure*'? Which might engage in each of the above behaviors?

Could an analysis that compares each of the three political categories to each of the behaviors discussed in *this* chapter be valid considering all the complications? Indeed it could be valid.

Is an analysis *feasible or desirable*? Maybe, maybe not. However, I believe that simply *labeling* folks as either '*liberal*', '*conservative*' or '*unsure*' doesn't really help us solve any problems. What *will* help is for each of us to know exactly whom we are up against, to recognize the uncivilized *behaviors* with which some will conduct themselves, avoid those who participate in *those behaviors* and avoid doing those same things ourselves.

And also things have become *way too* complicated. There are indeed way too many existing '*rules*' to address. There are way too many opinions being thrown around as facts. There are way too many deceitful and manipulative people out there with their own agendas. There are way too many criminals, way too many who '*just react*' or make decisions based on '*how they feel*', way too many who work for our way-too-big government who in turn take way too much from the '*haves*', and there are way too many people who don't '*think*'.

So what do we do? There's only one option. We simplify. We eradicate all of the '*way too many*' and '*way too much*'.

Does that mean that we eliminate people? No, but we do indeed need to eliminate from the decision making process all of the liars, cheats and thieves, as well as all of the saboteurs.

We must work only with those who have proven themselves to be honest, sincere, and truly working for a civilized society.

We must adopt the 'K.I.S.S.' method, the 'Keep It Simple, Stupid' method.

We need to *fix* things. We need *real* solutions that *really* work. We need *more* people to '*think*', or *learn* to '*think*'. *Only then* can we move towards our '*civilized society*'.

Continuing with the categorizations of '*liberal*' and '*conservative*' could help us simplify by stereotyping people into one of two groups. Stereotyping is a very common method that our brains use in order to more quickly process our thoughts. But this shortcut may only help to maintain friction between the two groups. There is already '*way too many*' and '*way too much*', and that includes way too much friction. For many, as will be discussed in Chapter 4, this friction is a desirable condition. But for expediting our ability to work together in order to find *real* solutions that *really* work, walls must be tumbled, the automatic friction that exists must be eliminated, and all other sabotaging behaviors must be identified, and avoided, too.

Chapter 3

Who Can Be Trusted?

Grandpa and Grandma on my Mom's side each came over from the old country. Grandpa escaped in the nick of time as a teenager about to turn the age for mandatory enlistment into the Russian Army.

I'm not certain at which of his 90 years he stopped trying to improve his mastery of our American English language. He spoke in broken English until the end reverting often to the Ukrainian that he learned as a boy, reading religiously the local newspaper that was written in Ukrainian. I found the broken English to be endearing. It added a twist to our communications with each other. We often had to find *other* ways to express ourselves in order to make our points.

Grandpa liked to tell stories and I loved to hear them. He and I would have a party. That meant that we would sit together on the back porch of their old large farmhouse with today's treat from either his garden or his orchard. He would sit with a bowl on his lap, a knife in his hand, and he would work at the strawberries, raspberries, peaches, pears, or apples, eventually stabbing them with the knife and reaching a piece to me. If I wanted to participate then I was required to remove the morsel from the end of his overly sharpened knife. Mom always lost her mind when she saw him doing this but her only relief was to leave the scene so that she couldn't *see* what was happening. Out of sight, out of mind. There was no changing Grandpa or the things that he did.

As we had our parties he would tell me stories. Of those stories there are three that are forever etched in my mind.

"Fool me once, shame on you. Fool me twice, shame on me." In our little world of struggling to communicate, *that* constituted a story.

We've all heard this bit of wisdom in one form or another. I'm forever grateful that I heard it in my Grandpa's broken English. He made it unforgettable.

"Dey fool da people" was another of his three stories. This was his most common story. He usually looked out into the distance and slowly shook his head back and forth as he spoke those four words.

And how right he was.

We've all done business with someone who in the end screws us. It's one of those inevitable learn-the-hard-way lessons that we all have to learn. It takes several of these experiences before we are finally able to learn how to judge someone's character right up front, and determine right off the bat whether we want to deal with this new person or whether he's likely to be one of those who tries to screw us.

This lesson is a critical one. A person has to protect himself. And how we respond to these screwballs is essential to our ability to keep from getting screwed again.

For me? Most of the time I will simply turn and walk away. I believe I would be wasting my time debating with that screwball. He knows he's like he is. How could he not know? A few poignant words aimed at him before I leave may be necessary. However, the ultimate solution for making sure that he never ever does me over again is to never ever deal with him, again.

Lawsuits? Get even? Perhaps they are necessary but those we'll leave for a different discussion.

Who can be trusted?

If we return to the many types of people that were discussed in the previous two chapters, the easiest groups to address are the liars, cheats and thieves.

Liars:

When someone has proven to you that he will lie, what happens when something *important* comes up that needs to be discussed? Do you really think that he can be trusted in the future? Whether he tells the truth during your problem-solving discussions, does what he says have any real value if he can't be trusted to tell the truth?

What about '*thinking*' through an issue along with a liar? The first requirement for '*thinking*' is the facts. However, lies are not facts. In fact, lies may even be the *opposite* of facts. Thus, if the liar introduces a lie as fact, and that lie is not detected to be a lie, then the entire process of '*thinking*' is completely compromised. Any '*thinking*' that *is* done will be meaningless and thus useless. Even worse, it could end up that any resulting solution is *completely opposite* a real solution that really works,

What about including a liar in helping to resolve problems in the political process? The result will be the same as discussed above. Any political discussions will be suspect, at best, and *completely* wrong at worst. Can you depend on a lying politician to solve a problem in a way that really solves the problem? Absolutely not. In fact, I believe any politician who has proven himself a liar should be automatically extricated from his political position. But our political system is completely upside down. We excuse politicians for lying, because, after all, he's a politician and he's got to make everybody happy. And I heard recently on talk radio that *it's not even against the law to lie in political advertisements.* Is this believable? Could this be true? Some of the folks who so many of *'the people'* put on a pedestal, look to as our *'leaders'*, and rely on to *'solve our problems'* are the *exact people* who should *never ever* be trusted; namely lying politicians.

Our legal system does indeed recognize the absolute necessity to tell the truth, to state facts. *"Do you promise to tell the truth, the whole truth, and nothing but the truth, so help you God?"* with your right hand raised and your left hand on The Bible. Perjury is a universally understood word.

Yes, yes, yes. I too remember the age-old joke. *"How can you tell when a politician is lying? His lips are moving."* Indeed that's funny the first time you hear it but it's only funny because it is so diabolically horrible in its implications. Does our chuckling over the joke make it somehow acceptable that politicians lie, because, after all, they all do? Or what about *'talking out of both sides of his mouth'*? Is this just another way that we convince ourselves to excuse the behavior?

Will I personally try to *'work things out'* with a liar, maybe somehow reach a compromise? Why on earth would I even consider doing so? He'll probably only lie again and the agreement will be moot. All agreements require a promise from each participant. A liar can't be expected to keep his promise while non-liars might. The liar's end of the agreement will likely not be met. Only *my* end will be met; I *keep* my promises.

Personally, I make a conscious decision to completely avoid liars. He has proven who he is. For my own safety and sanity, I avoid him like the plague.

Politicians are people who we hire to perform specific jobs for us. If the politician lies then he cannot be trusted in that position. If people are going to politicians for solutions to their problems, any lying politician will be a person least able to arrive at a real solution that really works. Yet the concept of *'lying politician'* is so pervasive that we have taught ourselves to overlook this flaw, to hold our noses when we place our votes, when conversely, *lying should be the most blatant and obvious reason for not being put into a position of power.*

We all need to develop my Grandpa's lie detector and to respond appropriately when it goes off.

"Fool me once, shame on you. Fool me twice, shame on me."

What about telling a little *'white lie'*? Indeed we all know that some lies seem insignificant and meaningless, so much so that we categorize these little gems as little '*white lies*'. But which lies are '*white lies*' and which ones are *real* lies? Is it meaningful to distinguish between the two?

If a little kid is in the process of growing up and has not yet learned the lesson about whether George Washington chopped down the cherry tree, and a harmless '*lie*' is told, then this '*lie*' becomes a forgivable '*lie*' and an opportunity to teach the kid a lesson about lying. But if an adult is telling the little '*white lie*' then your antennae should go up. Any adult who has no problem telling little '*white lies*' may also have developed a callused ability to indulge in *full fledged* '*lies*', too.

'*Keeping secrets*' can often fall into the category of little '*white lies*'. What if no one gets hurt over the little '*secret*'? What if a person is just protecting one's self, what-they-don't-know-won't-hurt-them, I-have-the-right-to-remain-silent, or I-plead-the-fifth? In many cases, folks will consider this '*secret keeper*' guilty of *something* although they may never know what the actual guilt relates to. However, if the secret is being kept because the answer is plain old nobody else's business then kudos to the '*secret keeper*'. Just because some ill-mannered person has the audacity to ask a specific question doesn't mean that an answer must be provided.

Some '*secrets*' are excusable. Folks who ask questions that are intended *only* to *hurt* the '*secret keeper*' are indulging in uncivilized behavior. Those people who ask questions that would be considered '*out of bounds*' in polite society participate in sabotaging our civilized society. We all have secrets. Few of us want our dirty laundry exposed to the scrutiny of others, and especially not to our political opponents.

However, there are so many people who are titillated by the dirty laundry of others. And there's money to be made feeding that titillation. But must we join in and indulge in this smut? Must we reward these purveyors of contamination? Not if our goal is a '*civilized society*'.

If no one gets hurt with the divulging of the secret *except* the '*secret keeper*' then chances are good that the answer *is* nobody else's business, thus kudos to the '*secret keeper*'. But if the secret is about someone other than the '*secret keeper*' getting hurt then the '*secret keeping*' most likely *is wrong* because it is intended to hide something that is quite likely truly relevant. *This* '*secret keeper*' *is* guilty. *This* secret is *no* little '*white lie*'.

'*Liars*', '*lies*', little '*white lies*', '*secrets*' and '*secret keepers*'… Absolutely don't put up with '*liars*', don't too easily forgive little '*white liars*', and in some cases allow '*secret keepers*' their privacy and mind your own business.

Cheats:

These folks are somewhat like '*secret keepers*' and somewhat like '*liars*'. These folks enter into an arrangement with one or more other people. The '*rules*' are known and it is assumed that each person in the arrangement will play by the '*rules*'. But the cheater breaks the '*rules*' and hides the fact that he has done so.

Take a monogamous relationship between two people, maybe even a marriage. The understanding of monogamy is clear. But when one of them cheats then the relationship is jeopardized and the cheated-on is victimized. Very likely the cheater will become a '*secret keeper*' and the '*lies*' told will be anything but little '*white lies*'. The cheated-on gets hurt, the cheater fights back, and the civility between the two vanishes.

Take a game of high-stakes poker. The one '*rule*' that each participant is ever vigilant about is in regards to each opponent playing by '*the rules*'. How severe might be the repercussions should a participant even be *suspected* of cheating?

How about the State Lottery? Surely the government can be trusted to not rig the games. You know, those bureaucrats who's jobs are protected, who get paid more than the average Joe, who's benefits and retirements are way beyond what most of us can even dream of getting. What if just one government official in a key position in the State Lottery system is a bleeding heart do-gooder who wants to make sure that only the underprivileged get the big payoffs? After all, every ticket sold is recorded, every set of numbers selected is stored in a computer, the location of every vendor who submits a bid is known. What if the key official could make sure that tickets sold to vendors who are located in *rich* neighborhoods *never* win. The selection process could be made. I've been a computer geek for twenty years. Don't think for a minute that this would even be difficult to do.

What if the key official was a racist? The key official may not want tickets sold in certain racial neighborhoods to ever win.

But no way, no how, this just couldn't happen. The government is holier than thou. The government could never do anything that could be construed as '*cheating*'. No single individual in the government, no one person, no key official, could be dishonest, right? We excuse the *elected* government employees for their dishonesty. But government employees who don't go through the intense scrutiny of an election? No way could any of them be dishonest.

And what about our *elections*? What if one key official...? Do you know how many news articles and even *books* have been written about election fraud? Do we really know who is writing those computer programs that count the votes? Do we really believe that everyone who has '*won*' an election has really '*won*' it, that no one has ever '*cheated*'?

Oh, oh. I've just caught myself indulging in '*what if*' behavior. Am I turning off my '*thinking*' in my efforts at '*what if*'? Emotions just like '*what ifs*' can be useful motivating factors. They can also help us to see potential pitfalls in *solutions* that we propose. '*What ifs*' can help us to analyze whether a solution will really work, help us to implement safeguards to protect ourselves from '*liars*' and '*cheats*', but the list of '*what ifs*' is so long and they diverge into so many different directions, that they must be reserved *only* for motivating us into action and verifying that our solutions are rock solid. They should *not* be used for identifying *new efforts* to be undertaken by our government.

Avoid cheaters. They can't follow the '*rules*'. Never accept their '*promises*' as anything other than noise. And never ever allow them into your government unless, of course, a '*civilized society*' is *not* your desire.

Thieves:

A decade ago I sat and listened while a youngish male neighbor of mine told me about some home repairs that he had done for another neighbor further down the block. An elderly widow lived in a big brick two-story house with her retired daughter. The story telling neighbor bragged about a tool he had taken from down in their basement. I carefully reprimanded him for his thievery. He slurred back at me that the old lady had millions, that she couldn't possibly spend all her money as it was, and that she'd never miss the old tool since it was a *workshop* tool and her husband was long gone.

Well, even overlooking the sexist ingredients of his comments, I determined at that moment that I could no longer be a friend of my story telling neighbor. I was literally dumbfounded.

That vulnerable elderly woman had trusted him in her own home and he had violated her. Whether she had more money than either of us could even dream of having at that stage in our lives, or whether she would ever notice the tool was missing, were irrelevant. A thief is a thief and they can't be trusted.

That story divulges several dilemmas. Some folks mentally justify stealing depending on *from whom* they are stealing. Rich? Yep, it's okay. Vulnerable? Yep, it's okay. No one is watching? Yep, it's okay. Some one trusted you? Too bad, sucker.

And these thought patterns are far too prevalent. How about sliding something small into your pocket at a retail store? How about taking supplies from your place of employment to stock up your home supply cabinet? Do folks really think that these activities are really okay? Is the *big corporation* an acceptable victim? Is it all okay if you don't get caught?

I'm astonished at the lackadaisical attitude that some folks have with regards to stealing. I can't do it. I won't do it. I will not trust anyone who *does* do it. And I won't associate with them, either, because thieves can't be trusted.

"They figure the loss into the prices they charge" is a typical excuse. So that means that the rest of us, whether we be fellow thieves or clean as newly fallen snow, will pay larger prices so that the thieves may indulge in their disgusting behavior. In fact the loss does indeed get passed along to the rest of us. But not just in the world of commerce. These situations present themselves in our government, too.

The whole concept of government is one that depends *completely* on passing the cost on to others. Everything that the government does is based on someone else picking up the tab. Certainly a government is necessary in our efforts to obtain a *'civilized society'*, and since the government can only function if it obtains money from those who actually produce something of value, sellable products or services, we taxpayers are inevitably saddled with having to pay the bills. However, where do we draw the line when it comes to what we would have the government do and how much of our money that they can confiscate? And who decides the limits on each?

It is very easy for me to view too many of the things that the government does, be it defining our laws or collecting their revenues, as thievery. Too many of our government officials, be they elected or appointed, exploit the same thievery thought patterns that are too common amongst the general public that I discussed immediately above.

Rich? Absolutely take from them, the more the better. *They* have more than they need. *They* can afford it.

Consider Robin Hood. He is held up as a hero, steal from the rich and give to the poor. But what most people don't remember is that Robin Hood was stealing from rich *government officials*, folks who didn't deserve their riches because they had been stolen from the poor in the first place. The Robin Hood story is *really* about returning what had been seized by government officials. That puts quite a different slant on that story.

How about the graduated income tax policy that has richer people paying a larger percentage of their income in taxes? Where did this idea originate? Let me quote:

"A heavy progressive or graduated income tax..."
is one of the ten planks for the implementation of communism, straight

out of *The Communist Manifesto*. Is this the philosophy that we want to emulate? During *my* upbringing, communism was considered a plague that had to be destroyed. So how is it that communist ideological thought patterns continue in this country? Are folks unaware of where their thoughts will lead? Or is something more sinister at work?

Vulnerable? Absolutely take from them. They can't put up much of a fight anyway. And who are the vulnerable? Folks who are old and decrepit, no longer able to put up a fight. They're sitting ducks. They can be exploited. Folks with physical disabilities. They too can barely fight back. And actually any person who is working hard, reaching their limit of exhaustion everyday, trying to meet all of the needs of their families, and who have no time left, no money left, no energy left, to take on another battle. They too are vulnerable.

Stealing from the vulnerable involves more than just taking their money or their belongings. It also includes stealing from them their sense of security, their self-assuredness, their hope in tomorrow. The truly repugnant in our government have developed a relationship of dependency between the government and the vulnerable. Then those same repugnant government officials threaten and accuse that the *other* guys, the *bad* guys, are going to take what little the vulnerable have left. And far too often, because of the dependency, the vulnerable are manipulated and the repugnant in our government win.

No one is watching? Absolutely take it while you can, before they notice, before you get caught. But remember always to *"fool da people"*. Don't call it *"taxes"*. That way they can be led off the scent. Call it a fee. Call it a permit. Call it a license, or a penalty, or several popular phrases of late namely *"contributions"*, *"government investments"* or *"government revenues"*. Just don't call it a *"tax"*. And how about writing more laws and more regulations that will keep those taxpayers moving so fast to try to feed the ever increasing appetite of the government that inevitably more people become vulnerable, and more and more vulnerable, until finally they too can no longer keep up and they seek help *from* the government. Now *those* folks are truly hooked; *those* folks are vulnerable.

Someone trusted you? Absolutely take from them. Someone trusted the government? Too bad, sucker.

Big corporations? Absolutely take from them. They are, after all, held up by some as a scourge on our society. They are the epitome of evil in that they exploit society by daring to make a profit when they produce something that people want to buy. And they make their employees work in order to actually *earn* their pay. And some employees are expected to actually work *hard*. Those corporations are greedy, they destroy our environment, they deserve to be punished, they deserve to pay.

And the bigger, more powerful, or more desperate that our *government* becomes, the more that they beat up on the corporations. Regulations increase, taxes increase, and the threats of penalties increase. The corporations respond by hiring more accountants and lawyers to fend off the onslaught. And some may even hire lobbyists in an effort to sway the actual laws being written. Ultimately the additional costs will be passed on to the consumer of the corporation's products or services. Or in the worst case, the corporation will pack up shop and move to a place where the level of regulations and taxes do not exist.

And *that* is the good news. All governments are not as oppressive as other governments, some government officials do not lean towards *bigger* government, and there are no requirements that government *be* oppressive. Government *can* be lean. Government *can* be limited. But much depends on what society expects of them, and what society will bear.

Things are not always clear cut when it comes to if and how government influences our complicated society. Everyone is looking for the best deal that they can get. And that's okay. That's what keeps many of us striving for something better. But the best deal is only fair when everyone involved is aware of the deal and approves of the deal. But when you get government involved then the waters get very muddy.

'*Playing the system*' is what many folks do. '*If you can't beat 'em, join 'em*' is a common strategy.

I've another close acquaintance. He brags about what a great guy he is because he's got millions, earned initially from his own small business but dramatically increased from wise investments. Although he's got all this money, he's got himself and his kids on the health insurance of his schoolteacher wife. Yep, he's getting himself a great deal, the best deal he could get. But the problem is that *not everyone involved in the deal approves of the deal.* It is people like me who are paying for his health insurance, me, a single childless taxpayer who cannot afford his own medical insurance. The best deal for my acquaintance is being paid for by the taxes that are coerced by the government. But I have little say in the matter. I just have to keep on paying my taxes so that the government can keep making their own '*special deals*' for their '*chosen*' recipients.

Everyone out there is looking for the best deal that they can get. Somewhere along the way it has become acceptable to take '*free*' money from the government without feelings of guilt with regards to whether we have *earned* the money. One of the best deals going is getting something for nothing, and when a check is received from the government then folks believe they are simply '*playing the system*'.

Welfare payments fall into those categories of '*something for nothing*' and '*playing the system*'. Didn't we learn, for instance, several decades ago that paying unwed mothers per dependent child only inspires the woman to have additional children in order to increase the payments that she would receive from the government? It is indeed a good thing to help those in need, and Americans are *very generous* when it comes to helping those in need. However, I question the wisdom of having the government involved in what could be accomplished though charitable organizations.

But let's not restrict our ridicule to just those at the low end of the economic spectrum. We've also all heard about corporate welfare and sweetheart deals that folks at the high end of the economic spectrum receive. Why on earth is our government allowed to pay off their friends, political associates and campaign contributors with special laws that provide special protections or special compensations simply because they '*know*' a powerful government employee?

Remember, all the payments being made are coming out of the billfolds of the taxpayer.

So how do we put limits on what government can do? We compose our '*rulebook*'. But we must abide by those rules otherwise those rules are useless and meaningless.

Where in our '*rulebook*' is it written that our government was allocated the power to demand money from the taxpayer in order for the government to make charitable contributions to welfare recipients? Whether doing so is a nice thing to do is irrelevant. As I've stated before, Americans are very generous and there are in fact numerous charitable organizations that can fill the desires of the benevolent contributors. What we are discussing here is *whether the government is following the rules* or whether they are out of control and are using their power to coerce their own desires in order to promote their own ambitions, feather their own nests, hang on to their power.

Where in our '*rulebook*' is it written that the relatives of government employees get special rates on premium medical insurance to be paid for by taxpayers even though those relatives could afford to purchase their own insurance and some of the taxpayers cannot afford their own cut rate medical insurance?

Where in our '*rulebook*' is it written that our government was allocated the power to write laws about anything that they can conjure up in their power hungry brains?

Just because our government does what it does, does *not* mean that the activity is a correct or advantageous activity. Just because the government is doing something that seems like a *'nice'* thing to do doesn't mean that they should be doing it. Just because the government has the power to take our money does not mean that the taking is correct or advantageous, especially if the government is doing things that our *'rulebook'* never allocated to them the power to be involved in.

The government forcing money out of our pockets in order to finance endeavors outside of their proper purview is nothing more than *thievery*. And *thieves* cannot be trusted.

So we now have analyzed the *liars*, *cheats* and *thieves*. What about *other* types of people in our society and whether *they* can be trusted? How about those people who are involved in **Twisting the Meaning of our Rulebook**?

<u>*Too complicated. It requires a lawyer*</u>:

The statement is false. Our *'rulebook'* is not too complicated. In fact, I'm amazed at how simple it actually is to understand, even after a couple of centuries. Go ahead and read it yourself. I've even included it as Appendix 1 of this very book. There are a few words that were spelled differently than they are today. There are a few phrases that may need clarification but that's because we are not as familiar with the document as we should be. Perhaps our schools should spend a semester reviewing our *'rulebook'* since it is such an important document. You may also need to slightly enhance your vocabulary but that's what a dictionary is for, just in case.

On the other hand, if it *is too complicated* for some then perhaps we should give no credence to the opinions of those who can't understand. After all, if they can't understand our *'rulebook'* then how can they justify opining on its content? Perhaps they shouldn't be allowed to vote? Just a thought, but perhaps it is also a solution.

And what about requiring a lawyer? Do you really trust lawyers? If you had a choice, would you put your future well being into the hands of a lawyer? Does our society really have a chance to survive if all is dependent on the views of lawyers?

Consider a most common view that we all have of lawyers in action as we might see on television, namely via a jury trial. We view at least two lawyers, the prosecuting attorney and the defense attorney. We start with presumably two divergent lawyer opinions, one of guilt and one of innocence. Ultimately each lawyer gives his opinion, presents the facts that he wants displayed, and then uses his ability at persuasion. However, it is the pool of *real* people, the jury, who are trusted with making the final decision, just as it should be. Here in these USofA we believe that *real* people *can* think, real people *can* see the truth, real people *can* determine whether someone is following the rules.

So why on earth would our '*'rulebook'*' be written such that *real* people couldn't understand it?

'*Too complicated. It requires a lawyer*' sounds like either a liar at work or a lawyer lobbyist attempting to guarantee employment for every lawyer that can be produced. Would I depend on someone who has this view? No, I wouldn't. Would I trust them? No, I wouldn't. I would suspect that those folks were trying to pull the wool over our eyes, to hide the rules by discouraging us from attempting to learn and understand them ourselves.

Am I badmouthing all lawyers? Absolutely not. We truly need a plethora of *good* lawyers. However, *good* lawyers would never hold the '*too complicated*' view. Perhaps this is one way to differentiate between the trustworthy lawyers and the non-trustworthy slime ball ambulance chasers.

Install judges who will write their own laws:

Our Founding Fathers knew that writing our rules was critical in our ability to reach for the best life possible for all in our USofA. However, they also knew that those who were writing the rules needed to be as close to the *real* people as possible in order to assure that the rules were the right rules. The officials in the House of Representatives would fit that bill best. Not only would each '*represent*' the smallest number of people per '*representative*' of any of the other officials defined in our '*rulebook*', but they would also be up for re-election every two years. If they were not performing as their constituents preferred then there would be another opportunity to replace them within a relatively short amount of time.

So adamant were they about who should write the rules that they stated their beliefs *twice* in our '*rulebook*', and also *first*.

> "Article. I. Section. 1. All legislative Powers wherein granted shall be vested in a Congress…which shall consist of a Senate and House of Representatives."

Then at the end of

> "Article. I. Section. 8. The Congress shall have Power To…"

and after listing all the duties of Congress, our '*rulebook*' states

> "To make all Laws which shall be necessary and proper for carrying into Execution…all…Powers vested by this Constitution in the Government of the United States, or in any Department or Officer thereof."

There seems no doubt about their intentions on this matter.

While I discussed above the House of Representatives and its relationship to the *real* people, the Senate is a little different. Originally the Senators were to be appointed by government officials from each separate State of the Union. This was supposed to make the Senators represent the well being of their entire State as a whole, each separate State being a very important entity in the scheme of the Union. However, after our efforts to rebuild ourselves after "*The War Between the States*" (or what is often referred to as "*The Civil War*" and less often to as "*The War of Northern Aggression*") and around the time of "*World War I*", someone apparently found that each Senator standing up for his own State was unworkable and the method for selecting Senators was made more "*democratic*" with the passing of the Seventeenth Amendment. (The discussions about these events still simmer as to whether this had been a good idea, but those are discussions that warrant further discussion elsewhere.)

So Congress is the only group of folks with the power to write law. However, those folks with an agenda will do whatever they can to impose their agendas on the rest of us. Considering all the methods of "*fooling da people*", if only we could get a single individual into a position of power, like into a judgeship, in a courtroom where the Judge is supreme, and were that one individual on *our* side of an agenda, then we could get him to '*twist the meaning*'s of our laws such that he changes the '*interpretation*' to mean something that the original law writers never intended. And his '*interpretation*' would stand until Congress finally got around to rewriting the law in order to clarify and/or correct the '*interpretation*'. But the chances of the same law writers still being in a law writing position, and the chances of them getting around to rewriting a law that they'd already spent so much time writing the first time around would be slim, especially considering all the more current and pressing issues that are on Congress' plates.

So in the end, a Judge's ruling can have the affect of writing a new law where one had never existed. And this, too, is against our rules. These individuals are not following our rules. These folks are pushing their agendas down our throats in a powerful yet '*cheating*' manner. They cannot be trusted.

Refer to the U.S. Constitution as a living, breathing document:

This declaration is one that I've heard numerous times. I am floored whenever I hear it. I cannot conceive how anyone can have this viewpoint. And when the declaration is made the person always exudes an air of flippant insignificance, implying that either the '*rulebook*' needs to change with the times, bend with the wind, or that what it says is hardly relevant.

But how can they think this? This document is a contract, signed by the U.S. government and each State as it joins the Union. States agreed to become States based on their acceptance of this contract. Not only is the U.S. Constitution our '*rulebook*' it is a legally binding contract between the U.S. government and the States. It cannot and should not be changed haphazardly. And what it states should be solid, a fortress, not namby-pamby.

So how can anyone be so flippant about it?

Perhaps these folks simply don't care which laws are laws. Perhaps they think that as long as *their* guys are in power then whatever laws are passed are okay with them. Whatever their beliefs, their Gumby backbone is one that I find disturbing.

Do I trust them? Not with *my* well being…

Imply that the U.S. Constutution says things that it does not say:

The example I gave the first time I discussed this '*twist the meaning*' issue is the most critical to the success or failure of our '*civilized society*', and it bears repeating. *We are not a democracy, we are a republic.*

A democracy is one where the "*majority wins*". For example, let's say that there are ten hungry cannibals. Nine vote to eat the especially delectable tenth. Bon appetite.

Democracy is often referred to as '*mob rule*' and '*mob rule*' seems a long distance from '*civilized society*'.

A republican form of government is often referred to as "*a government of laws, not of men*". That means that our laws are *not* based on what any particular man decrees but on laws that are written and passed legislatively. Our laws are indeed *supposed to be* written legislatively. If done in this manner and if people adhere to the laws, our '*rulebook*', then we're giving it our best effort to reach for our '*civilized society*'.

Another discussion for this '*twist the meaning*' issue comes to mind:

Implications can be very devious. Some politicians use them profusely. A common claim is that people have certain Rights that the government has a '*responsibility to provide*'. The implication is that somewhere it is written that these "*Rights*" have been granted and that it is somewhere written in our '*rulebook*'.

Our Founding Fathers identified in the *Declaration of Independence* that

"…all Men are created equal, that they are endowed by their Creator with certain unalienable Rights…and…to secure these Rights,

Governments are instituted among Men".

In the USofA we are born with Rights because we are human beings. Governments are there to "*secure*" those Rights. My *Merriam-Webster Dictionary* defines "*secure*" as "*free from danger or risk of loss*". That definition is a far cry from '*responsibility to provide*'.

> "Amendment IX. The enumeration in this Constitution of certain rights shall not be construed to deny or disparage others retained by the people."

Indeed people have Rights but it is *not* the responsibility of the U.S. government, nor its politicians, to identify what those Rights are. And regarding what the government could or should be *providing*:

> "Amendment X. The powers not delegated to the United States by the Constitution, nor prohibited by it to the States, are reserved to the States respectively, or to the people."

So if a U.S. politician tries to have the U.S. government provide anything that is not spelled out in the U.S. Constitution, then that U.S. politician is out of bounds. However, the State governments *can* promise to provide things (that are out of bounds for the U.S. government) should any of the States choose to do so.

Should we trust people who imply that our '*rulebook*' includes items that it doesn't implicitly state? Well, *they* are just another group of *liars*.

Keep the people stupid:

This '*twist the meaning*' issue is perhaps the most far reaching of all of the '*twist the meaning*' issues, as well as a fact on which all of the *liars*, *cheats* and *thieves* depend. If '*the people*' don't realize that they are being lied to, manipulated, or led astray, then the chances are better that they will be unable to mount a successful fight against whatever it is that the government is trying to pull on them. The more the number of people who don't know how to *think* then the larger and more oppressive the government can become. The fewer the number of facts that are supplied to the few remaining who *can* think, then again, the more oppressive the government can get away with being.

And these facts have been known for a long time. Consider the days of old, was it ancient Greece or ancient Rome?

'*The people*' were consumed by '*the games*'. Those '*games*' might consist of a bunch of healthy athletic young men competing in sporting events. These healthy athletic young men would compete in the nude. That made for huge turnouts for sporting events in those ancient times. But don't you think that the turnouts would be just as huge if conducted in the same manner in today's USofA?

Those '*games*' might *otherwise* involve prisoners subjected to ferocious animals '*in the ring*'. The results were predictable. Huge numbers of spectators came to watch the blood bath.

And who is it that financed these '*games*'? The politicians, because they knew that if '*the masses*' were otherwise entertained then they, the politicians, could do as they pleased. Those politicians appealed to the emotions of '*the people*'. The brains became disengaged and the emotions became triumphant when their sights were on human bodies being devoured by gnashing teeth or solid torsos with floppy appendages performing in the wide open sunshine.

Today's '*people*', as in ancient times, are being otherwise entertained. There is no shortage of people consumed by sporting events. There is no shortage of people consumed by Hollywood and all that they produce. There is no shortage of people who would rather do *anything* than to know and understand what our government is doing.

Certainly those in our government would prefer that *no* one was watching. No one likes someone else constantly looking over his shoulder. However, most of us have a boss and that is the boss' job, to watch over his hired help. And reality is that politicians are *our hired help*. They are employed by each of us taxpayers. And many of them *need* to be supervised.

Those who are doing their jobs will react most calmly to the watchful eyes. They understand that the boss has got to do what the boss has got to do. However, those who *aren't* doing their jobs or have something else to hide will squeal as if you just stepped on his tale. The good employees will sometimes even appreciate your involvement, your interest in what they are doing, and your personal quest for additional knowledge. The bad ones will resent you, and where you are sticking your nose, and they'll squeal even louder.

But don't think that you can't be entertained while watching our politicians, even when compared to watching our sporting events or Hollywood productions. Reality can be far more amazing and entertaining than fiction. You will find it hard to believe the things that are said and done when you lift the rock and the government squealers start to scurry around.

Do all politicians want you stupid and/or unaware of what is going on? Not the good ones; and these good ones *can* be trusted. But the rest of them? Those who want you stupid? Don't trust them for a minute.

In the previous chapter I spoke momentarily about our schools and how they can be used to perpetuate a populace who cannot think for themselves and to permanently instill an automatic response of looking to the government whenever a problem arises. Our schools are indeed a crucial topic and they warrant another comment here.

Many who seek power also recognize the important role that the schools play with regards to preparing our next generations. But what are they preparing them for? Another quote from a source referenced numerous times already, the quote being:

> "Education of all children, from the moment they can leave their mother's care..."

This is another of the measures identified for installing communism, straight out of *The Communist Manifesto*.

Do I keep referencing and quoting this document because I have a paranoid fixation on there being a communist under every bed? Not specifically. However, those who justify doing '*whatever it takes*' may have adopted certain thought patterns that are self-destructive. History has proven, facts have proven that communism doesn't work. So why do people keep thinking in these terms? Is it because they are communists? Or have they simply not used their brains for any purpose other than for manipulating the masses using ideas that *sound* good on the surface but don't prove successful for anything other than placing the idea person into a position of '*power elite*'.

In the 1990s there was a wife of a U.S. President who claimed credit for writing a book titled *It Takes A Village*. From that book she launched a campaign to convince the masses that it would be especially beneficial for government to install mandatory government-run *preschool* for every child in this USofA. There were many who saw this as another attempt to grab on to our children at the youngest age possible in order to start the pro-government indoctrination process at the earliest point possible which would solidify the government's role in the thought patterns of all in the coming generations. The campaign failed but don't be surprised if it resurfaces.

Do I trust anyone who voices communist beliefs? Hell no! Do I trust anyone who tries to keep people stupid? Dah.

The commerce clause and for the general welfare:
Here we have the keys to the kingdom; the pot of gold at the end of the rainbow; the answer to every power hungry politician's dreams. Any politician who is worth his salt should see the endless possibilities in these two phrases and should be able to twist them to suit any nice-sounding idea that he might stumble upon. However, I wonder if any of them have ever considered that "*the general welfare*" might be best served by considering each individual's personal welfare resulting from *more personal freedom*

and actually fight for *smaller* government, *less* regulation, *fewer* taxes, and *simpler* rules? How deep into the bottomless pit must we dig ourselves before government turns the corner and starts to downsize?

In our *Declaration of Independence* our Founding Fathers identify '*liberty*' as one of our unalienable Rights. In today's language '*liberty*' is pretty much synonymous with '*freedom*'. Although I truly believe that our '*general welfare*' is best served when '*freedom*' is maximized, I have no faith that any of the politicians who utilize either the '*commerce clause*' or '*the general welfare*' clause to justify their latest and greatest proposal have *more freedom* in mind. Thus, at this time, I believe each of those politicians is looking to again increase the government and all that that involves. So will I trust these particular politicians? You guessed it, no I won't.

Write so many laws that no one can possibly read them all:

Let's say that you get a knock on the door. You answer and find outside a couple of suits with badges from either the IRS or the FBI. Even if they announce that they are '*here to help you*' is there any one of us who wouldn't immediately get a sick feeling in their stomach and a heart that starts pumping double time? Your mind starts racing, flooding with thoughts about why these people are here? What could I have done? Has someone accused me of doing something? The list goes on.

There are now so many laws out there that it is conceivable that each one of us, no matter how mundane our lives, is possibly breaking some law, be it obscure, out-of-date, whatever, that have accumulated over time. Most of us don't want to believe that we could be breaking a law, but how are we to know? We are told, "*ignorance of the law is no excuse*". Are we all required to *become* lawyers just to have a running chance?

Is it possible that our USofA could simply collapse from the weight of all the laws that currently exist? Could Washington D.C. sink into the Potomac River due to all the piles of files? Perhaps it is time for someone to start digging through all the '*older*' laws that currently exist and start putting them up for a vote of Congress to eliminate them. That could help us eliminate lots of laws we no longer need (whether they actually served a good purpose at some previous time) as well as keep Congress so busy that they couldn't pass any additional laws.

Some laws of late have been passed with a "*sunset*" clause. That means that unless a renewal of that law is passed at some future date, the law will automatically become void simply based on the passage of time. That's a great idea that should be included in *more* laws.

What some folks consider a horrible condition sometimes occurs when one party controls one portion of the elected U.S. government while the other party controls a different portion of the elected U.S. government. They call the condition *'gridlock'* when the two groups cannot work together enough to actually get laws passed. From my point of view *'gridlock'* is the one of best things that can ever happen. When Congress passes laws it is usually to the detriment of *'the people'*. As I've stated before, passing laws to *eliminate laws* or to *increase our freedoms* isn't what many politicians seem interested in doing. So unless things change dramatically, I don't trust most of the laws that are being passed nor most of the politicians that are so busy passing them.

Written by a bunch of rich, racist, white males a very long time ago:

This view is one that I find especially disgusting. It can only be held by someone who is himself racist or sexist. Not everyone limits their opinions of others based on one's looks or physical traits with which one was born and cannot change. Those of us who *'think'* appreciate others who *'think'* regardless of their physical appearance. Those who *don't* think are more likely to hold non-thinking racist or sexist views.

White males are just another category of individuals with some who think and some who don't. Could some of them be racist or sexist? Certainly. But is racism or sexism mandatory for being included in the group? No, white males are white males due to accidents of birth.

A natural and normal human trait is indeed to *discriminate*. Everyone must pick and choose between numerous alternatives everyday. Discriminating between the different options is what helps us get a better bang for our buck, more for our money, and *not* discriminating can cost us big. Discriminating is a necessary tool we humans must develop. But being a discriminating individual does *not* mean the person is racist or sexist.

The reference to *'rich'* is one used to stir up the deep dark emotions that everyone is capable of feeling, those of jealousy and resentment. For those people who *don't* think, feelings reign supreme and feelings can be easily manipulated by having their deep dark emotions fed. But for those who *do* think, they may even admit that they too would like to be rich, many aspire to become rich, and they certainly don't want the government getting in the way in their efforts to acquire their riches.

There are despicable people who try to earn their riches by seeking ways to throw fuel on fires that dwell deep inside each of us. We all indeed have fears. Situations abound for which each of us questions our ability to deal. Fear of the unknown, if not addressed, can cause all sorts of inner turmoil. And when someone tries to capitalize on those fears, working to keep the different types of people divided, accentuating the occasional odd ball and using him to try to prove that *all* people who share certain physical or economic traits with the odd ball are likely to behave in *all* ways like the odd ball behaves, is outrageous. These promoters of unrest use the blame game to justify to their followers why their followers are in the predicament that they are in. It's somebody else's fault. It's those rich people. It's those white males. When in fact it is more likely the fault of non-thinking people. Then these promoters of unrest attempt to become *profiteers* of unrest by appealing to those folks with access to more money than anyone else, namely the government, appealing for special treatment, appealing for reparations, playing on the feelings of guilt or fear that those in the government may possess. These *profiteers* of unrest are working to sabotage any progress being made at attaining a '*civilized society*' by promoting unrest. These profiteers are thus the enemy of those who seek a '*civilized society*'. These profiteers, some of them quite possibly racist or sexist, must be ignored. They must *not* be trusted.

And regarding the fact that our '*rulebook*' was written a long time ago, that those ancient authors couldn't possibly have anticipated today's issues, I say hogwash. Human nature is human nature. Humans were humans two hundred years ago. And humans are humans today. Those ancient authors did a phenomenal job with their compositions. They had a clear understanding of how oppressive an out-of-control government can be. They were in the midst of the Revolutionary War. They wanted to place limits on what government could do. They wanted to tie the hands of the government. And that is indeed what they set out to do with the writing of our '*rulebook*'. But somewhere along the way the rules seemed to have changed. The rules *now* tie the hands of the citizens, the businesses and the people themselves. The government seems to be able to do whatever it wants to do as long as they can use the media to convince all the citizenry that '*something must be done*' and that the government is *naturally* the ones to do it. If anything, our Founding Fathers did not tighten the shackles on government enough.

Ignore certain words or interpret words to mean one thing in one phrase but something different in another phrase:

A fascinating dilemma that faces we humans is our ability to process into our beings contradictory information. Selfishness is bad; we should learn to share. Selfishness is good. If *we* don't worry about *ourselves* then *who will*? Somehow we take it all in and even if the input claims that polar opposites are both true, we somehow sleep on it, deal with it, fight within our own selves, and then move on. But we never really resolve the contradictions; we simply learn to live with them.

There are many people out there with an agenda. In fact, most of us at one time or another *is* motivated to go out and fight for what we believe. The problems often arise when those with an agenda would insist that their agenda be imposed on others, by law, by force. However, the *good* fight usually seems to be from those who battle for *'just leave us alone!'*

Those who would impose their agenda on the rest of us have discovered the above method of exploiting the fact that many of us suffer from accepting contradictory inputs. They use the method as simply another way of selling their ideas, for manipulating the masses, for demanding that *they* get what *they* want.

But in the end, science proves that there is only one set of facts. Contradictions only exist because not all of the facts have been gathered or presented.

Proving one's point can be far more successful if one leaves out certain crucial words from their quotes of others when presenting their arguments, that ignoring certain words dramatically alter the meaning of their quotes, so they conveniently overlook those nuisance words.

Ultimately, these folks are in essence misrepresenting the truth. They are misleading in order to manipulate. They are in fact *lying*.

So if you want to allow others to use their *lies* to impose their agenda, then go right ahead and let them. Otherwise, if you *'think'* that *liars* should *'just leave us alone'*, and *you* get the itch to stand up for yourself then please consider climbing aboard the *good* fight.

Change the meaning of words in our current language:

Words mean things. Words have enabled our society to move past grunting animals, to form thoughts, and to communicate with one another. As society becomes more sophisticated, so do our words, and the greater one's vocabulary then the better equipped he is to think his thoughts and communicate them to others.

But also as society changes, we play games with our words, especially the younger sect of people and their slang inventions.

The word "*cool*" is one such word whose slang interpretation has taken hold so permanently that it has lasted through numerous generations. No longer is it just a temperature between warm and cold. Now it also implies a commendable level of societal attractiveness.

Another such word is "*marriage*". I believe it once represented a lasting commitment between members of the opposite sex, a promise made before God, a natural situation for attempting to guarantee the successful perpetuation of our species.

Then somewhere along the way the government got involved. They began issuing licenses, then granting divorces, and in between bestowing special benefits to the union between husband and wife. Eventually even the meaning of some phrases in our '*rulebook*' were changed in order to accommodate the married couple:

> "Amendment V. No person…shall be compelled in any criminal case to be a witness against himself…"

The oneness between husband and wife suggested that a spouse should also not be compelled to testify against the spouse. And this way of thinking is now pretty much set in stone.

Time passed, society became more complicated, and benefits for the married couple grew. Businesses joined in by providing special gifts for the spouses of their employees including such things as insurance policies for medical expenses and survivor benefits. But naturally the cost of these gifts had to be paid for by others. The denying of these same gifts to those who were not married helped to fray the costs, but the non-married soon recognized that they weren't being treated as generously as their married peers.

Now a current idea sweeping the country is discussion of "*gay marriage*". The purpose of these '*unions*', as I see it, is simply for single individuals who claim to have made a personal commitment to another person of the same gender to cash in on all of the freebies being handed out to their married peers. And the way they plan to cash in is by changing the meaning of the word "*marriage*" when in fact they are just another group of people with an agenda, another group of people who see others getting something for nothing and they too want in on the takings.

Can I blame people for wanting the best deal that they can get? Again, no, but altering the meaning of the word "*marriage*" in order to accomplish their goal is another insidious method for imposing their agenda. What they *really* want is a piece of the socialism pie, rewards even though they have not endured a marriage and all that it entails, something for nothing.

But can socialism and freedom co-exist? Or have we another dilemma or contradiction?

Call for a Constitutional Convention:

Although this option is not really '*twisting the meaning*' of our '*rulebook*', anyone who thinks that our basic '*rulebook*' is so unworkable that it must be trashed in one fell swoop has something in mind that cannot possibly include "*freedom*" nor the "*protection of our freedoms*". The basic '*rulebook*' is a good one if only folks would *follow* the rules.

However, many of the laws that have been added since the original *'rulebook'* may quite likely be detrimental to either our *'civilized society'* or to our *'freedoms'*. I won't trust anyone who suggests a Constitutional Convention.

So there we have it, a long list of the types of people who cannot be trusted. Although the list is long, I believe that the number of people who *can* be trusted, the *real* people, is much, much larger. But the desire of many of the *trustworthy* people to place themselves into the jaws of the U.S. government, whether by joining the ranks of elected officials, by becoming a bureaucrat, or by simply being noticed by the any of them, is tremendously lacking. Who would really want to debate issues with *liars*, *cheats*, or *thieves*? Who can't see the futility in trying to convince the lying, cheating and thieving rivals to *'think'*, to *'be honest'*, to work for *'what is best'* for this USofA? Who won't admit that reaching a compromise with those untrustworthy adversaries will only tarnish our own clean records and move us deeper into the *'liberal'* abyss?

Is there a way to build a force field around ourselves in order to protect ourselves from the leviathan? Is there promise in our futures that we will someday be able to call the head of security in order to request that he *'raise the shields'*? Maybe our only option is to bury our heads in the sand, playing ostrich, in order to not see what we all are in for if we don't turn this behemoth around? Maybe keeping the truth *'out-of-sight thus out-of-mind'* is our only defense, that if we ignore them then maybe they'll ignore us. Or maybe that's why we are in this mess because too many of our ancestors ignored what was going on in the U.S. government, too busy in their own lives, too trusting that the U.S. government would do what was best, or simply themselves attempting to stay *'out-of-sight thus out-of-mind'*.

Trustworthy people need our help. Future generations need our help. Our *'civilized society'* needs our help.

Chapter 4

Keep Them Divided

I can blame *no one* for being turned off by politics when you consider what we must watch and listen to about some of our politicians. I am not surprised that many folks want to steer clear of the whole darned ugly mess.

However, regardless of what our media tells us, regardless of which views they present as desirable and which as less than desirable, which political party that they say is good and which is bad, which individual politician is like a gift to our society and which is evil incarnate, we *really must be* concerned. Because like it or not those politicians will affect us, our lives, our billfolds, and our ability to survive.

My *Merriam-Webster Dictionary* has as one of its definitions for "*politics*": "*competition between groups or individuals for power and leadership*". Those folks who are allowed into positions of power *will indeed* lead the country in *some* direction. Do you want a say into which direction we head?

The U.S. President who held office during the earliest years of the 21st century came into office claiming determination to make Washington, D.C. a place where the two political parties would '*get along*' with each other, would '*work together*', that a new era of '*cooperation*' would be forged. He insinuated his sincere desires to truly attempt this feat by *not* replacing large numbers of attorneys and department heads who themselves were replacements installed by the previous President of the other political party. But did this show of '*good intentions*' influence a more cooperative result?

From the outside looking in it appears to have made no difference at all. Previously existing attitudes continued, business as usual. The opposing political party immediately went on the attack alleging the complete incompetence of our newly elected U.S. President. And throughout his years they never let up.

Was it the opposing party's fault that the cooperation never materialized? Were they correct in their assertions about the President's lack of ability? Were *they* refusing to '*get along*' because forging that cooperation would have placed a feather in the President's cap and that simply could not be allowed to occur (since the President was of the opposing political party)? Or perhaps there were some authentic conservative bones in that President's body and he had added things up and recognized that compromise with certain types of people will only result in digging us deeper into a liberal abyss and further away from the conservative goal? Or maybe all this friction was just a smoke screen so that *none* of us could possibly keep track of what was really going on in Washington, D.C.?

From my point of view, the President seemed always to conduct himself in a kind and civil manner. But that's hardly the way that his opponents described him. Thus in the end his civility was never acknowledged by his opponents in the other political party nor by their allies in the liberal media organizations. And was that inevitable? I believe that indeed it was. Because many folks on the political scene believe that it is in *their* best interests to '*keep us divided*'.

There seems to be two distinct methods of discourse in Washington, D.C. One is more calm, considerate, non-imposing, non confrontational. The other method is aggressive, accusatory, intimidating, demanding and demeaning. Folks who are sincerely '*nice*' perform the first method. The folks who act '*nice*', who prefer to not '*make a scene*', who don't want to '*upset*' others conduct themselves in a polite and mannerly way. The *other* folks see this '*nice*' behavior as a sign of weakness. They view it as an invitation to storm the seemingly weak, helpless prey and verbally eat them for lunch.

The '*nice*' officials may quite likely come from the ranks of people who believe the government should '*just leave us alone*'. The '*not so nice*' people most likely believe in '*whatever it takes*'.

On the surface it may appear that the '*not so nice*' people win the battles when it is only *their* voices that seem to get heard. They do make the most noise, create the biggest raucous, give the cameras a more exciting show. But if they are doing so as described above, namely via aggressive, accusatory, intimidating, demanding and demeaning behavior, then they border on being uncivil. The battles that *they* win, or lose, have certainly not moved us closer to our civilized society.

But those folks with the good manners, whether they win or lose, will have at least *tried* to reach towards civility.

These two methods of discourse between the '*nice*' and the '*not so nice*' continue on, year after year, decade after decade. The '*nice*' continue to be '*nice*' even though their supporters might wish that they'd add a little more pep and vinegar to their debates. And the '*not so nice*' continue to stoop to dirty street fighting in order to get their way. The perfect atmosphere is created to '*keep us divided*'.

Do I expect these realities to change? I wouldn't hold my breath.

I spoke in Chapter 3 about folks who I referred to as profiteers of unrest. These '*not so nice*' politicians that wouldn't '*get along*' were simply performing the same disruptive act, perpetuating unrest. They apparently believed that there was profit to be made by *not* '*getting along*' or '*going along*' with the President. Most likely it was *political points* that they sought to gain; and at what cost? Civility, at least.

But their *real* motive was to sabotage most anything that the President might accomplish. They wanted him to be perceived as a failure, especially since he was truly succeeding at several of his endeavors.

His tax cuts resulted in repeated record revenues arriving into the U.S. government coffers. But tax cuts are antithetical to a liberal's belief system. To them taxes are good. They can be used to manipulate behavior of the masses. They can be used to purchase votes. They can be used to punish one's enemies. But record breaking amounts of money in their coffers? Now *that* was a good thing, too. But a President for the opposition political party getting credit for making so many people happy? Taxpayers paying fewer taxes? Government spenders with more money to potentially spend? And the President getting the credit? The opposition would look good. That just couldn't be allowed to occur!

That same President *also* made our country *safer* by responding with commitment and strength to those who had masterminded the worst attack on U.S. soil, namely the toppling of the twin towers in New York City. So many in this country rallied behind him. So many came together with a single purpose, namely to retaliate against the evil enemy. Another horrible catastrophe for a liberal, a country *not* divided. So *that* must *also* come to an end!

Ultimately the profiteers of unrest *did* succeed somewhat in their efforts. They succeeded in influencing "*surveys*" to show that the masses *did not* approve of the President's conduct. They succeeded in creating enough noise to suggest that the masses were dramatically split. Daily discussions between individuals within the general public did indeed display discomfort, confusion, and opposing beliefs. And how did the profiteers of unrest finally accomplish all this?

The USofA had declared "*War on Terrorism*". Much of this '*war*' was conducted as militaristic action in the country of Iraq. Regardless of the shoulds and shouldn'ts of having gone in there in the first place, one thing is for sure; eventually, if not instantaneously, '*war*' will divide the masses.

So many discomforting events occur during war. The most obvious horror is that people die, or are maimed for life. There is so much suffering. Horrible things happen to "*women and children*" (those people who are always thought to be the most innocent and most defenseless). Boatloads of money are spent in the effort. Our hearts become overfilled with sorrow and anxiety. We can only imagine the pain and devastation being experienced by those people so far away.

But this "*War on Terrorism*" wasn't *only* being conducted in lands far way. One purpose of the militaristic actions in Iraq was to attempt to focus the efforts of our enemies to one of the places where terrorists were harbored and nurtured, a place outside of our USofA. But we'd be foolish to not suspect that the terrorists were *also* still at work on our *own shores*.

Let's dwell a bit on this topic of '*war*'. It is such an important issue that it warrants some intimate discussion.

Note that during '*war*' different rules apply than those that apply when *not* at '*war*', at least this is so in *our* country.

Note also that the Rights guaranteed by our '*rulebook*' apply to citizens of the States of the USofA, and of the U.S. territories, including Washington, D.C. They are *not* guaranteed to anyone else. Do others want those guarantees? No doubt they do, but sorry, that's one of the perks of becoming a citizen.

> "Amendment IV. The right of the people to be secure in their persons, houses, papers, and effects, against unreasonable searches and seizures, shall not be violated, and no Warrants shall issue, but upon probable cause..."

Per the "*War on Terrorism*" our government participated in monitoring phone calls and emails in order to acquire knowledge regarding potential terrorist activities in the planning stages. They claimed also that they only did this against individuals who were not citizens or when the phone call or email extended outside our USofA.

The profiteers of unrest caused lots of raucous, calling these invasions of privacy, warrant-less searches. Without question any blatant disregard for the Fourth Amendment should not be tolerated. And based on my own lack of confidence in the integrity of some individuals in our government, I'll be first in line to call foul. However, we are at war, the guarantees are for citizens, and besides I'm certain that there are laws that have been passed for '*exceptions*' during times of war. But do I really trust our government to do what is right? Well, for the sake of our civilized society, I'm going to *have to* believe that enough checks and balances are indeed in place that will keep the monitoring from being abused. But am I a dolt to believe this?

"Amendment V. No person shall be held to answer for a capital, or otherwise infamous crime, unless on a presentment or indictment of a Grand Jury, except in cases arising in the land or naval forces, or in the Militia, when in actual service in time of War or public danger..."

This Fifth Amendment did a better job of spelling out the exceptions for times of war.

Also during our "*War on Terrorism*" potential enemies of our country, folks suspected of having terrorist connections, were placed in internment camps outside of the 50 States for interrogation purposes. And you can be sure that the profiteers of unrest boisterously accused the U.S. President (of the opposition party) of imprisoning these people unjustifiably, with no proof, with no indictments, and they even claimed that they were being treated inhumanely, even being tortured. But as above, we are at war; the guarantees are for *citizens*, etc, etc.

"War is horrible!" "People are dying!" "We shouldn't be over there!" "Bring our troops home!" The chorus of voices against the war were repeated time and again by the media who agreed with what these voices were saying, or at least in helping the liberals present the President as a failure.

But did everyone climb on board the bad mouthing of the President? No, because *some* people think.

It is also important to point out a few more details that our Founding Fathers found it crucial to include in the original '*rulebook*'.

"Article. II. Section. 1. ... The President ... Before he enter on the Execution of his Office, he shall take the following Oath or Affirmation: - "I do solemnly swear (or affirm) that I will ... to the best of my Ability, preserve, protect and defend the Constitution of the United States."

There is little left to the imagination based on the above quote. The U.S. President takes an oath at the moment that he begins his term, to preserve, protect and defend the U.S. Constitution, or in other words, these USofA.

The U.S. Congress (the U.S. House of Reps and the U.S. Senate) take a similar oath although their version was modified and expanded during the "*War Between the States*". It now reads:

"I do solemnly swear (or affirm) that I will support and defend the

Constitution of the United States against all enemies, foreign and
domestic; that I will bear true faith and allegiance to the same;..."
Any doubt about whether there may actually be enemies within our borders,
from time to time, was obviously contemplated and eliminated. As with
the U.S. President, the U.S. Congress *must also* do their darnedest to
protect us from our enemies, even if these enemies are within our borders,
even, I assume, if that means '*war*'. And as a side bar:

"Article. VI. ...the Members of the several State Legislatures, and
all executive and judicial Officers, both of the United States and the
several States, shall be bound by Oath or Affirmation, to support this
Constitution;"

The oath of office is not limited to just the U.S. President and the U.S.
Congress.

Few of us *like 'war'*. But as long as we have enemies '*war*' may be
a necessary evil.

The topic of '*war*' always resurrects in me all of the repetitious
thoughts that I've had since reading a particular book several years
ago. That book presented some amazing views. The book was indeed
controversial. Some claimed that no one ever came forward and verified
that the contents of the book were factual. However, even considering that
claim the mere fact that this book was published is enough justification for
me to contemplate its contents. The title of this book is *The Report From
Iron Mountain On The Possibility And Desirability Of Peace*, and it was
published by The Dial Press.

This book has not gone unnoticed. An example of what the
"*establishment*" had to say about the book can be seen in a newspaper
article that someone had photo copied and slipped into my copy of this
book prior to my finding the book at a used book store. That article was
from *The Wall Street Journal* dated May 9, 1995 (while the copyright date
of the book was 1967). This article had been on the front page, above the
fold, in the top most left corner of the page. In other words, the editors of
the *WSJ* gave the article the most important and prominent spot in their
newspaper that any article can receive, a spot where the likelihood that the
most people possible would see and read the article. Obviously *someone*
saw the importance of responding to this book even though *nearly 30 years
had passed* since the book had been published.

The *WSJ* article used some 2100 odd words to make their case that
the book was a hoax. Throughout the article words were chosen carefully
to suggest the ridiculousness of the claims that the book makes, suggesting
the credibility gap of *anyone* who would believe such a book (as is typical

of any discussion that attempts to sway the views of the readers), etc.

However, two points made in the article did especially catch my attention. According to their descriptions, I believe that I have an authentic original version of the book as opposed to one of the counterfeit versions that were apparently published at later dates.

Secondly, one quote from the article enforced the thoughts that I had after reading and rereading the book. The introduction in the book is written by a Leonard C. Lewin. In that intro he claims to be passing on a report written by a specific "John Doe". The *WSJ* article quotes a 1972 essay in the *Times Book Review* (the book having made it to the *New York Times Bestsellers List*) in which Mr. Lewin had simply hoped to

> "pose the issues of war and peace in a provocative way … perhaps, with luck, to extend the scope of public discussion of 'peace planning' beyond its usual stodgy limits."[1]

In other words, in both his words and mine, the topic of *'war'* is indeed a topic worth consideration, discussion, and a thorough analysis.

Why would I give any credence whatsoever to a book that the *WSJ* has reported was a hoax? Undoubtedly *someone* is trying to *'fool da people'* but was it the *author* or was it those in power at the *WSJ*?

I attempted to learn more about the author in order to give to or take from his credibility. A Google search resulted in tens of thousands of potential "*hits*". As I dug through them I soon found that the author's main claim to fame seemed to be this "*Iron Mountain*" book, he being a graduate of Harvard University, a writer from New York. However, there were a small handful of entries that also credited him with being a "*critic and satirist*" who was editor of *A Treasury of American Political Humor*. Indeed this didn't do anything to add to *his* credibility but instead it reinforced the view of those in power at the *WSJ* as someone to *not* be taken *'seriously'*.

One particular Google entry struck my fancy as it stated a few things that are worth quoting. That entry came from *The Silver Bear Café* and included the following excerpts.

"… in language full of think-tank jargon …"

> "The report caused panic among many government officials. President Johnson supposedly "hit the roof" when he learned of it. Cables were sent to U.S. embassies throughout the world instructing them to play down the public discussion of the report, and to emphasize that the report had nothing at all to do with official U.S. policy."

> "Even though Lewin … admitted that the report was a hoax, there still remain some who believe it to be an official government

document that was leaked to the public."

So where does all this leave *me*?

Knowing that there indeed are people who seek power, knowing that some of them will do anything to gain and retain that power, and considering that we are discussing a topic as consequential as '*war*', I cannot just tell myself that "*It's just a hoax. Forget about it*". Because as the years pass by and I see all the news that makes the news, I am repeatedly reminded of the contents of that book and how neatly certain news items could fit into the concepts that are written of in that book.

Do I believe the book? Well, I believe that it is worthy of contemplation ...

In order to respect and protect the integrity of the author's arguments while also not infringing on his copyright protections, I will carefully select a very minimal number of excerpts from his book in order to attempt to convey his message. But I'll also emphatically recommend that you might seek out and read the entire book so that you can yourself consider the entire message.

The *Foreward* of the book includes the following explanations:

"... Its objective was *to determine, accurately and realistically, the nature of the problems that would confront the United States if and when a condition of "permanent peace" should arrive, and to draft a program for dealing with this contingency.* ..."[2]

"... the Special Study group ... met and worked regularly for over two and a half years, after which it produced a Report."[3]

What supposedly happened was that the U.S. government commissioned 14 professionals, each an expert in a different field such as one of the sciences, business, academe, etc. and who also "had done work of distinction in two different fields"[4]. The team was to meet secretly for as much time as was required in order to compose a secret report.

A couple of excerpts from the body of the book describe the findings of the Special Study group:

"... the war system provides the basic motivation for primary social organization ... it reflects on the societal level the incentives of individual human behavior. The most important of these ... is the individual psychological rationale for allegiance to a society and its values. Allegiance requires a cause; a cause requires an enemy ... the enemy that defines the cause must seem genuinely formidable ... the presumed power of the "enemy" sufficient to warrant an individual sense of allegiance to a society must be proportionate to

the size and complexity of the society. Today, of course, that power must be one of unprecedented magnitude and frightfulness. ...”[5]
“... However unlikely some of the possible alternative enemies we have mentioned may seem, we *must* emphasize that one must be found, of credible quality and magnitude, if a transition to peace is ever to come about without social disintegration ... in our judgment ... such a threat will have to be invented ...”[6]

Then finally a summarization of their conclusions:
“... Lasting peace, while not theoretically impossible, is probably unattainable; even if it could be achieved it would almost certainly not be in the best interests of a stable society to achieve it. ...”[7]
“... Some observers ... believe that ... the price of peace is, simply, too high. ...”[8]

Indeed the excerpts are cryptic to understand, but I'll rephrase and summarize the message for you.
In order for a government to keep their society '*in check*' there must be a grandiose '*enemy*' that justifies the government's control of the masses. As long as that enemy exists people will put up with governmental oppression. For those who believe that people *need to be* controlled and that government is the solution to all of life's problems and that society can only survive if government defines what is right and wrong and then the general public is somehow forced to comply with what the government demands, then the ideas in the “*Iron Mountain*” book can be used to justify *anything* that a government does, even the most vicious and cruel activities imaginable, for the good of society. (And to quote a tiny number of the despicable “*options*” that the book proposes as possible substitutes for war, consider the following.)
“... reestablishment of slavery ... the *deliberate* intensification of air and water pollution ... universal test-tube procreation ... the long-range planning – and “budgeting” – of the “optimum” number of lives to be destroyed annually ... is high on the Group's list of priorities for government action”[9]
Like I said above, despicable.
But for those of us who believe that individuals can become self reliant, competent and responsible adults who can take care of themselves all the while respecting the rights of others, the *ideas* in the “*Iron Mountain*” book help suggest what may be the reason behind the ever-growing insidiously manipulative leviathan that the government has become and that must be carefully dismantled.

The *"Iron Mountain"* book suggests that *'war'* is pretty much inevitable in the world in which we live. Reviewing history, it appears indeed that when one war ends another seems to be waiting in the wings. There also seems to be many in our government who are ready and willing to go to war and plenty in the general public who are willing to enlist to fight those wars. And actually, that's a very good thing; because as long as there are those out there who are ready to *'attack'* us, we must be ready to *'defend'* ourselves.

There are also many in our government, as well as in our general public, who, for all the obvious reasons, are completely *against* *'war'*, no matter what. They seem willing to wear their blinders, refuse to see *'attacks'* from our enemies for what they are, unwilling to do anything but *'talk'* with those who have *'attacked'* us, try to *'reason'* with them, try to *'understand'* why they are so *'upset'* with us, and try to *'negotiate'* with them. Haven't we already discussed the complete use*less*ness of negotiating with certain types of people? Maybe these *'enemies'* themselves *also* believe in the use*ful*ness of war as described in the *"Iron Mountain"* book, that for the sake of *their own* society, in order to maintain control of *their own* masses, that our enemies must have *their own* enemies. And who better than the USofA to fit that bill?

But then, maybe we in the USofA *are* responsible for aggravating our enemies to the point where they *'attacked'* us in the first place. Who can say what some in our government may have done in lands far away in years gone by? Can we really know? Can we really be sure?

Finally, as for the USofA's military being used as the world's policemen? Used for making the rest of the world safe so that international businessmen and international vacationers can travel worldwide with minimal fear, as the *"globalists"* desire? I'm all for exporting freedom, I'm all for defending ourselves, and I'm all for retaliation after we've been attacked, but is that what's really going on?

And something else worth considering: was it not a former U.S. President who warned us to *'beware of the military/industrial complex'*?

Some are all for *'war'* and some are dead set against it. But *'what if'* we could end all wars?

A slow and methodical analysis of just the excerpts that I've selected and included from the *"Iron Mountain"* book, when compared to *'issues'* that are thrown at us each day, make it seem plausible that there are non-warrior government officials who are aware of and believe in what the *"Iron Mountain"* book suggests.

In order that I don't spend any additional time repeating myself, nor wander too much further off point, I won't perform that comparison here. I will leave it to you to reread the excerpts and consider today's issues. But one quick comparison is worth the effort in order to prove my point.

Wouldn't *"global warming"* fit the bill for the perfect enemy, one so grandiose that it cannot be beaten down? The best that any one of us can do to fight this enemy is to join together, hope, pray, sacrifice, and, of course, allow the government to continue with all of their oppressive endeavors, like increased taxes, increased regulation, using their power to stay in power, all because *we must do something to fight this hideous enemy*! Even though the real facts show that human beings are hardly significant enough as residents of this planet to affect it as the *"global warming"* alarmists would have us believe. (But what about *nuclear weapons*? Now *they* are something created by humans that indeed could destroy life-as-we-know-it on this planet. But *nukes* also fall into the *"war"* category, thus they are not an acceptable *"enemy"* for the non-warrior tribe. However, if our *real* enemies are threatening us with *nuclear weapons*? Perhaps there really are things that are worth '*war*'ring over.)

Are the two options posed by the *"Iron Mountain"* book the *only two options* there are? Either we continue '*war*' or we find an enemy that can replace '*war*' and all of the economic, political, sociological, ecological and cultural needs that '*war*' fulfills?

I, for one, believe in the abilities of human beings to *not need* government to control us. I believe that so many people have already proven, based on their individual accomplishments, that not only could we survive without an omnipotent all-controlling government but we instead could thrive and prosper. Our country didn't become great because of our government controlling us but *in spite of* it, *before* it became so omnipresent and oppressive.

I believe in freedom, and the hope, promise and opportunities that it provides, if only we humans were allowed to spread our wings and soar. And government *must not* introduce too many excessive impediments to our efforts to strive for better lives but instead it must restrict *itself* to only those activities that protect us so that we can concentrate on our own self improvement.

Finally, to return to the more specific topic that this chapter set out to discuss, namely to '*keep them divided*', I am repeatedly reminded by watching the media that some in our government (and their friends in the media) spend an inordinate amount of time and effort pointing fingers at those in the opposing party, or lumping "*them*" all together and accusing them *en masse*.

Each time I hear these types of accusations I'm also reminded of recent news stories that described one or more of the accusers being guilty of the very things that they were accusing their opponents of being guilty of. Along with the memories of these news stories I often see the absurdity in the accusations that they were actually making, their lack of facts, the flimsiness of their details. I see that often they were accusing their opponents of their *own* crimes.

I remember the little ditty about how, when you point your finger at someone else, there are three fingers pointing back at you; the point being that accusers may be guiltier than the accused of the very things that the accusers are accusing.

I also recall that in Chapter 2, after composing my list of the "**Top Eleven Methods for Twisting the Meaning of Our Rulebook**", I admitted that I had a problem composing such a list because I don't '*think*' like a deceitful government manipulator. I believe this accusatory behavior to function the same way…

"It takes one to know one"…

"Do as I say, not as I do"…

"Actions speak louder than words"…

The secret of the magician is to keep you busy watching his *left* hand while his *right* hand is busy doing something that he doesn't want you to notice…

How many ways do I need to say this?

The accusers are really doing nothing more than functioning as '*profiteers of unrest*' and attempting to '*keep us divided*'. My advice is to do your best to *ignore* what these people are saying and figure out what it is that they are doing with their *right* hands.

Being '*divided*' is actually a natural human condition. Every teenager will sooner or later be *at odds* with his parents or other adult authority figures. Every teenager needs to rebel against the '*establishment*' that surrounds and restricts him. These efforts to grow into adulthood help to enable each teenager with adult strength and know how. Without these rebellious actions it is questionable as to whether the teenager will turn into a *real* adult.

At another level of '*division*', it is *also* quite natural for individuals to feel more comfortable and safe with people that are most like themselves. Family members will feel more comfortable and safe with other family members; they do, after all, share the deepest of all physical traits, namely genes. Men will feel more comfortable with other men and women with other women. Kids will gravitate to other kids. Members of one race or ethnicity will relax more readily with other members of that same race or ethnicity. These are natural conditions. People often prefer the *'easy'* way, and it is *'easier'* to *'adapt'* to those people who require you to *'adapt'* the least. However, the comfort and safety felt does not imply the inability or lack of desire for *different* types to get along with one another, too.

But it is *unacceptable* when these differences between individuals are exaggerated and exploited for political purposes, such as to *'keep us divided'*. That division stifles another natural human instinct, that of curiosity. And stifling that instinct can cause some of us to never strive beyond our own small lot in life which in essence eventually, if continued, repeated and/or increased, will kill the human spirit. And if you break man's spirit you will end man's desire to work for a better world. (Just take a look at what happened in the communist Soviet Union.)

So let's count the ways that we can be divided, and kept divided, for the benefit of the *'profiteers of unrest'*:

- The haves versus the have nots
- Black versus white
- Smokers versus anti-smoking zealots
- Gay versus straight
- Men versus women
- The elderly versus those young whip-per snappers
- Pro-life versus pro-abortion
- Average/moderate people versus animal rights activists
- Average/moderate people versus environmentalists
- Average/moderate people versus etc. etc.
- Republicans versus Democrats
- Our team versus their team
- Warmongers versus Peaceniks
- Socialists versus capitalists
- Etc. etc.

There are so many ways for us to be divided. Are we going to be their puppets? Are we going to allow ourselves to be manipulated? Are we going to fall for their shenanigans again? Will we allow them to continue to *'divide and conquer'*?

Or will we seek the *freedom* that so many of our ancestors came over to this country to find, the *freedom* that so many have fought and died for?

Chapter 5

Centralized Versus De-centralized

During my two decades of working I.T. (Information Technologies) departments of corporate America, I functioned more often as contract help as opposed to fulltime employee. This enabled me to experience far more '*situations*' than did the more typical white collar worker. However, during this time I was still a fulltime employee of a consulting firm. I was thus able to enjoy the best of both worlds, not being a job-hopper while still able to '*move on*' when I had finished my contract '*project*'.

At one place, contracting in a huge centralized corporate-level I.T. department, my boss was finishing up her Master's degree by having just completed the writing of her Master's thesis. She explained her paper as the "*advantages of globalism*". While I kept my own views to myself, knowing that talking politics at work can be very dangerous, especially for a contractor, I showed keen interest in reading her composition. I *was* sincerely interested to hear some positive views on the matter from someone who had apparently thoroughly thought it through. But alas, I never got to read her paper.

Over that particular eighteen month contract there were numerous other opportunities to talk politics since that was during the time when a U.S. President was impeached. And although I continued to bite my tongue, one particular time I thought it safe to respond to something that my boss was grumbling about. The encounter went something like this:

"It would sure be a lot better if all the laws were all the same in all the States in this country"

she opined.

"I can't believe that we have to adapt our business practices to all those different laws. There should be *just one* set of laws."

Wow, did I ever need to respond to *this* one, and as I stated above, I thought that I could do so safely, by just frittering around the edges. So I chose my words carefully.

"But that's one of the coolest parts of the whole country. Those guys way-back-when laid it out this way on purpose. The idea was that every State could try something different. Some ideas would be better, some would be worse; some ideas would work, and some wouldn't. The best ideas, the ones that *really* worked, would be observed by the other States and those other States just might adopt those same ideas, tweaking them a bit for their own State, trying their own hand at building a better mousetrap having allowed a lot of the trial and error attempts to be performed by previous States. The whole country could function as one big laboratory with different experiments going on simultaneously. Sooner or later the best ideas would be found. But that could never happen without each State having the freedom to experiment its own way."

I received only a snarling stare back at me when I concluded my enthusiastic discourse. I was met with stone silence until she finally got up and walked away. She never did respond to what I had said. Perhaps I had gone too far to describe my view on this topic. Perhaps she had expected me to just agree with her, to just be a good "*yes man*".

Perhaps I could have agreed that consistency in the rules could make adapting to them easier. Perhaps I could have pointed out that on the other hand that any company would have an advantage were they able to adapt to all of the different laws, an advantage over those companies who were unable to adapt.

And I wondered if she'd considered that if the one set of rules were *bad* rules then adapting to them might be even worse than adapting to the variety of rules that currently existed.

Maybe that day I destroyed the mutually respectable relationship that I thought we had established. I probably should have kept my mouth shut *that* time, too. Clearly I was frustrated from having bitten my tongue so many times before that I simply had to finally *say something*, to voice my own opinion. Eventually each one of us *has to* be allowed to speak our minds; otherwise we'll burst from the pressure. But oh well; that contract position is now just water under another bridge.

I began my description of the above contracting assignment as one in a "huge centralized corporate level I.T. department". That description is important to note. I experienced a very small number of *those* types of situations. I found that I could be far more successful and satisfied when I worked in *smaller* shops where I was located in very close proximity to the customers (users) for whom I was upgrading their software.

Those folks in the huge corporate level I.T. departments, who sit in the ivory towers, far from the real worker bees, far "*above*" the lower level or blue collar workers, don't ever quite understand what those "*lower*" workers really need in order to help them do their jobs. The ivory tower residents are far more likely to "*tell*" the "*lower*" folks (instead of "*ask*") what they need. "*Asking*" would apparently somehow be akin to admitting some deficiency in the knowledge and ability of the ivory tower resident, and ivory tower people simply cannot allow themselves to be viewed as having any form of deficiency.

I excelled in the places where I was allowed to work alongside my customer. We put our heads together, we debated the pros and cons of our options, we settled on what we could agree would be the best solution, I developed the software and my customers always ended up very satisfied, sometimes ecstatic.

I recognized the two different environments early on in my I.T. career. There were the *"Big Blue"* shops, those departments that ran huge IBM mainframe computers. Those departments seemed far more concerned about building fiefdoms than about actually delivering clean efficient product that truly met the *"user's"* needs. The *"Big Blue"* shops were huge sized bureaucracies with reams of red tape. However, they *do live* in spaciously extravagant ivory towers.

Then there were the departments that ran *"mini-computers"*. These machines usually belonged to non-I.T. departments, located out in the *"user"* community. The users owned and operated their own boxes which gave them total control and avoided all the pitfalls of the oppressive ivory tower bureaucracies.

In the I.T. business there was a big difference between centralized versus de-centralized. And as the years pass, more and more personal computers with more and more capacity and capability infiltrate our entire world. That dispersion of computers is putting more knowledge and more power in the hands of more people than ever before. The internet has increased that knowledge and power by leaps and bounds. More people are being empowered with enough information that they are able to make their own decisions about more things than ever before.

But the sophistication of the computer systems along with the internet could *also* result in enormous *centralized* monitoring of all the digital transactions occurring of what people *think* are private communications in the privacy of their own homes or offices. The tools that enable dramatic dispersion of knowledge and power might actually provide additional tools for the *control freaks* of our society to watch what we are doing. (And I'm not being paranoid, I'm being realistic. Like I said, I've been there...) There will always be people who prefer centralization and all that *it* can provide, such as power over other people. And if there's a will, there's a way.

We've all played the game *"telephone"*. One person tells a story to another person, who repeats the story to another person, and so on, and so on. Ultimately, when the last person repeats the story for all to hear, chances are that the story is quite different from the original story. The more the number of brains through which the story must pass, the more distorted the story becomes.

Now imagine that those brains are on different levels of a bureaucratic pyramid. Considering the predictable results of our *"telephone"* game, you tell me whether the decision makers who are so many levels away from us are even going to *"hear"* the same *"issue"* that we need to have discussed. And if the issue gets distorted, how valuable will be the response we get (if we ever *get* a response) once the response too re-travels all those brains at all those different levels and it finally returns to us?

I thought again about that ole' boss of mine and her desire that there be only one set of laws; isn't it obvious that the most likely way for those laws to be consistent throughout the USofA is if they were written in the ivory towers of Washington, D.C. and that the chances of those laws being good, effective, efficient laws that actually accomplish the best and most desirable results are slim at best? Didn't she realize that the further away the decision makers are from those who need a decision made, the less chance there is of even being *heard* much less actually having the actual issues addressed?

I recently wrote a two page letter to the Supervisor of the township where I live about a "city planning" issue that was recently in the news. Within a few days the Supervisor called me, left me voice mail, and invited me in to discuss the issue further. I was delighted that my understanding of how this country is supposed to work proved itself, again. I've chosen a responsive town in a responsive county (although the State where we are located is rather oppressive). The chances of my being able to communicate directly with the *"big boss"* were I living *else*where, or if the government *wasn't dispersed*, would be *much less* than it is.

Over a decade ago I ran for State Rep as a third party candidate, for the "Libertarian Party". A local high school teacher invited me in to speak to his government class about *"libertarians"*. Before I spoke I read the single paragraph in the class textbook that spoke of *"libertarians"*. That gave me the springboard that I needed. The encounter went something like this:

> "Your textbook describes libertarians as folks who are against government. It's really too bad that they say that because that's not at all what we believe. Instead, what we believe is that government is better when it is closer to the people and that government should only be doing those things that it was commissioned to do.

"By '*closer to the people*' I mean de-centralized. Your chances of walking down to city hall, rapping on the Mayor's door, and then actually getting to sit down and speak with him are a whole lot better than thinking that you're going to fly down to Washington, D.C. and actually get in to speak with the U.S. President. Besides, what are the chances that people in Washington could possibly know and understand the issues of our own city, nor why should they really care since they don't live here, or anywhere around here. This country is supposed to be "of the people, by the people, and for the people". It thus also needs to be *close to* the people in order to be effective. And it needs to be worth our while to get involved, too. One voice in a couple of hundred million voices is pretty darned meaningless while one voice in our own city does indeed have a chance to be heard.

"Secondly, regarding '*the government should only be doing what it was commissioned to do*': you may have noticed my campaign slogan. *"The U.S. Constitution and the First Ten Bill of Rights. The finest freedom definition ever published. Let's start using it again!"* Pretty bold, wouldn't you say?

"We as States *hired* with our tax dollars the U.S. government to do only a handful of things for us. Coin our money, protect us… Go ahead and read the U.S. Constitution. You'll see a rather small number of items. And now look at us today. Let's take that one item *"protect us"* and ask the question '*Are we protected*'?

"Can our police do much more than *simply respond after* crimes have been committed, *after* it's *too late*. Can our jails and prisons house all the criminals that are convicted in our courts or are dangerous criminals receiving early release in order to make room for the newest batch of felons? Is the flood of illegal aliens, including some who are sworn enemies of our country, being reversed, stopped, or even slowed down? Are we protected?

"Washington, D.C. is *not* doing what we *hired* them to do. But that doesn't mean that they are doing *nothing*. In fact just the opposite. Is there *anything* into which the U.S. government does not stick its nose?

"Then more specifically regarding the line in my slogan that states *"Let's start using it again!"* Take for instance last year; Congress and the President passed the largest tax increase in history. Not only that, they made it retroactive back several months to the first of the year. Now when I read the U.S. Constitution I see the phrase *"no ex post facto law will be passed"*. That specifically means that laws can't be passed that apply to the past. But they did it anyway. They made the law retroactive. Doesn't that prove that they no longer are following the rules that were set down for them? Is there any question as to whether they have overstepped their bounds?

"Another example that might hit closer to home, at a local level, for all you high school students:

"You probably have heard about our local school district pushing for adding to the graduation requirements for high school a semester of '*mandatory volunteerism*'. Our U.S. President has suggested it as a great idea for building community involvement for all in our country.

"Well, I attended a School Board meeting last month when this issue was supposed to be discussed along with a request for input from the community. Several people got up to voice why they thought the idea was a good one or a bad one. I don't think that the Board was being swayed by arguments pro or con. The Board was determined to make their U.S. President happy. So I stood up and gave it a try:

"I remember being in high school and I'll bet there are *some* things that *never* change. High schoolers find nothing more satisfying than identifying hypocrisy in the adults around them. Our schools teach that the U.S. Constitution is the supreme law of the land. In the Thirteen Amendment it states "Neither slavery nor involuntary servitude" and then you folks implement '*mandatory volunteerism*'. Besides the fact that the phrase '*mandatory volunteerism*' is an oxymoron, it's not much of a stretch to think that students would see hypocrisy in the two phrases '*no involuntary servitude*' versus '*mandatory volunteerism*'. So I say '*Go for it!*' Go ahead and implement your '*mandatory volunteerism*'. You think that you have problems *now* with young adults and their lack of community involvement? Just wait and see what happens when a few bright high schoolers wrap their brains around *this* one."

The class listened intently and numerous questions were asked of me. It was an invigorating discussion we had that day. The students all seemed quite geeked as they funneled out at the end of the hour.

And by the way, the '*mandatory volunteerism*' was eventually defeated by our local School Board. The de-centralization of school matters enabled our community to fight back against what a different U.S. President at a different time might have tried to implement by passing a law at the national level.

And since that time, the *next* U.S. President (of the opposing party) created a brand new *Department of Education* at the national level. Does anyone suspect that someone has '*centralization*' in mind?

And have you yet noticed that *my* stories are a bit longer than my Grandpa's stories?

Certainly there are arguments regarding the advantages of some situations or organizations being centralized as opposed to de-centralized. Otherwise, the idea wouldn't be suggested as often as it is.

Besides '*consistency*' in our laws as discussed above, the most often heard explanation is for "'*saving money*". Now "*saving money*" is a great idea *especially* if the money saved is money that would otherwise be pried out of *my own* billfold. "*Saving money*" could come about in several ways.

Centralization will usually include consolidation. For example, purchase orders that are written in multiple de-centralized locations could be centralized and consolidated. We all know that when you make purchases in larger quantities that you usually can save money. Purchase orders could be written for large quantities instead of lots of separate purchase orders with smaller quantities. The assumption is that the price would be lower per item due to the size of the large order.

Secondly, administrators who *write* purchase orders could be centralized and consolidated. Instead of having administrators in multiple locations writing purchase orders for the very same items, you could have a set of centralized administrators writing fewer purchase orders for larger quantities to supply the same multiple locations.

Fewer administrators should result in saving money.

Fewer purchase orders should result in saving money.

Larger quantities should result in saving money.

However, a single purchase order also means that all the items will be delivered to one location, when those items still need to be forwarded to all the multiple locations. Suddenly you have to develop a distribution process to move the items out to the different locations. You must now spend money on distribution.

Also, the centralized purchase order administration and the distribution process will result in requiring additional bureaucratic red tape. More red tape means less efficiency and extra work. Less efficiency and extra work costs money. All the savings that you thought you might find from centralized purchase order administration may be nothing more than a shift of the costs from one cost '*bucket*' into a different cost '*bucket*'.

So centralization doesn't always result in cost savings. In fact, let's look at it from a scholastic point of view.

My guess is that every Business major at the University is required to take ECON 101. In that class there are numerous concepts and phrases that are discussed. Without digging deep into discussions of microeconomics, there are two phrases that can come in handy here for our discussions of *'centralization'* in order to *"save money"*.

On the *'capitalism'* side of things there is a phrase, namely *"economies of scale"*. A short explanation of this phrase (as quoted from an economics textbook) could be: *"with infusions of grand technologies, large-scale production can result in dramatically reduced cost of production"*. Each ECON 101 student is taught that when producing on a large scale it is quite possible that the cost of each individual item can be dramatically reduced. And that means *'saving money'* and *'centralization'* of production is quite likely the first step in that process.

If we then fast forward through our ECON class we'll eventually arrive at another phrase that applies to our discussion, namely *"the point of diminishing returns"*. A short explanation of this phrase (from the same economics textbook) could be: *"in the process of increasing production, there is a point when costs stop being reduced and instead begin to rise"*. In other words, if you think that increasing production, going faster, producing more, will keep increasing your profits, you are mistaken. There is a point where profits stop increasing at the same rate and start to grow less quickly, if not actually start to *cost* you money.

And why is it that this can happen? For instance, in a manufacturing environment there might be numerous reasons. The machinery may begin to wear out and breakdown due to increased load. These breakdowns will invoke additional costs: the cost to repair the machines themselves, the cost of employees getting paid to stand around waiting while the repairs are being made, and the cost of the lost revenue due to time passing with no product being produced.

Increased production might also cause employees to become less focused on the jobs they are doing due to their own fatigue from trying to keep up to the increased pace of the production machinery. To avoid this increase of employee fatigue additional employees might be hired to spread the work more reasonably between more workers, but that creates additional employee costs and it might result in all the employees becoming less efficient because they all start to get in each others' way.

Finally, additional production could result in the market becoming saturated with an over abundance of product who's prices must be reduced, or placed *"on sale"*, in order to move them off the shelves (or in other words the basic laws of supply and demand). These *"sales"* will result in less revenue generated per each individual item and thus, again, a decrease in profit.

Another *"size matters"* discussion has been clearly described in a popular #1 national bestselling book called *The Tipping Point* by Malcolm Gladwell, first published in 2000. Gladwell devotes an entire chapter in his book to what he refers to as the *"Rule of 150"*. His *"Rule"* goes a long way to reinforce my argument that bigger is not always better, in fact quite the contrary.

In order to respect and protect the integrity of the author's arguments while also not infringing on his copyright protections, I will carefully select a very minimal number of excerpts from his book in order to attempt to convey his beliefs. But I'll also suggest that you might seek out and read his *"Rule of 150"* arguments directly from his book.

One of the many endorsements that preface the body of his book says a lot:

"In a fascinating look at research from the disparate fields of anthropology and business, Gladwell makes a convincing case that there is actually a magic number – 150 – beyond which human groupings become dysfunctional.'

- Gary Kenton, *News and Record* (Greensboro, NC)"

Within his book Gladwell builds on the declarations of a "British anthropologist Robin Dunbar"[10]. Gladwell discusses much of Dunbar's work and the following two quotes do an adequate job of summarizing those discussions. The first is a quote of Dunbar directly.

"The figure 150 seems to represent the maximum number of individuals with whom we can have a genuinely social relationship … the number of people who you would not feel embarrassed about joining uninvited for a drink if you happened to bump into them in a bar."[11]

The second is a discussion by Gladwell of Dunbar:

"Dunbar has combed through the anthropological literature and … he looks at 21 different hunter-gatherer societies for which we have solid historical evidence … and found that the average number of people in their villages was 148.8."[12]

Then Gladwell conducts numerous studies of his own. One such study is summarized as follows:

"Then there is the example of the religious group known as the Hutterites, who … since the early twentieth century, in North

America … (who came out of the same tradition as the Amish and the Mennonites) have a strict policy that every time a colony approaches 150, they split into two and start a new one."[13]
And his studies also included corporate America:

"Perhaps the best example of an organization that has successfully navigated this problem is … a … high-tech firm based in Newark … that makes the water-resistant Gore-Tex fabric …"

"Wilbert "Bill" Gore – the late founder of the company … stumbled on the principle by trial and error. … "People used to ask me, how do you do your long-term planning … And I'd say, that's easy, we put a hundred and fifty parking spaces in the lot, and when people started parking on the grass, we know its time to build a new plant." " [14]

Gladwell also discusses other types of social situations and experiments that he himself has conducted, pointing out again and again what he refers to as the *"Rule of 150"*.

For my efforts at including all these *"Rule of 150"* discussions here in *my* book, I am simply attempting to show again that bigger is not necessarily better and Malcolm Gladwell has helped to make my case.

So in our discussion, indeed size matters. However, *bigger is not always better*. And building a bigger *'organization'* as a result of *'centralization'* will *not* always result in *"saving money"*.

In this chapter you may have noticed that I have begun to suggest methods, via examples of things that I have done, for how a person can get involved in politics *other than* just going out to vote, *without* doing *'whatever it takes'*, and *without* becoming *'uncivil'*.

I've also shown that there are concepts that apply in the business world that can also be applied to the world of government. However, remember that business and government are two very different creatures. One requires that something of value be created and provided while the other can provide only if it has forcibly *taken* from someone who *has* something of value.

Lessons you learn in your day to day life, whether they are learned on the job, at your school, amongst your peers or group of friends, or elsewhere, are lessons that can be adapted to the political world. Becoming a clear thinker is one of the first and most important lessons of them all, but then so is honesty, integrity, consistency, stability.

So with all of this in mind, let's journey off into some mind expanding *'what if'* thinking. But beware, let's not participate in *'what if'* paranoid hand wringing. Let's not get worried and fearful. Instead, let's just see where this '*centralization*' business could send us in the world of politics.

> "Amendment X. The powers not delegated to the United States by the Constitution, nor prohibited by it to the States, are reserved to the States respectively, or to the people."

Remember, our Founding Fathers wrote into our U.S. Constitution the whole concept of '*de-centralization*', although not in so many words, and with *very few* activities '*centralized*'.

There currently exists a United Nations. From my point of view, it's a fine idea to have a safe place where representatives from all the countries of the world can go to *discuss* issues that many different countries have in common, and to come to some sort of agreement on what each country might do regarding their relationships with others. However, for the U.N. to be anything *other than* a speakeasy is dangerous to our USofA.

There are many people both within our country and elsewhere who have wanted the U.N. to become much more than a speakeasy. Repeatedly there have been calls for some type of '*world tax*' to fund the U.N. and the endeavors that *some* want it to become involved in. There have even been discussions about it having its own military.

If either of these events should occur what is expected is that every country in the world would become subservient to the U.N., even our own USofA. Some would say that that would be quite acceptable and perhaps even desirable. But I have great reservations about that. The idea undoubtedly is generated by those who believe in the superiority of '*centralization*' over '*de-centralization*', of one grandiose government having power over every human being on the planet and over every other government on the planet. I for one see the superiority of the USofA and its form of government (even though I *am* very dissatisfied with so many of the things that it currently does).

Consider all of the politics that are played today. Think of all the disgusting behavior of politicians today. What about all the corruption in government that we know of in our own country, today. And then think about how out of control things will become when we are talking about a government that is even larger, even more powerful, and even more far away. Do you really think things could improve with additional '*centralization*'? Do you think our lives in this country would remain as is, or improve, if a more omnipotent government was installed? Do you think that our U.S. Constitution could survive were the USofA subservient to an even more grandiose government?

Even though most in our country would not believe that the U.N. is a threat to our USofA at this time, it is worth considering how things would change if it *were to become* more powerful, if the U.S. government were to allow or even allocate additional '*centralized*' responsibilities to the United Nations.

My point here is *not* to discuss the United Nations except to consider that it has been proposed as the ultimate in '*centralization*' and '*consolidation*' of government. I have also included in Appendix 3 of this book a paper that I wrote as part of my campaign literature back when I ran for State government. It indeed makes some interesting points about '*centralization*', '*de-centralization*', and the U.N., but is presented simply as a bit more information on the ideas that we are discussing in this chapter.

Another idea that's been floating around out there, although it has only been mentioned occasionally here and there on radio talk shows, of both liberal and conservative slants, is the idea of a "*North American Union*". There are reporters who say that the U.S. President has already signed documents of agreement with the Prime Minister of Canada and the President of Mexico to "*merge*" our three countries into a single entity, with a single currency, the "*Amero*", etc. Is this possible? Is this really so far fetched? After all, many of the separate countries in Europe have joined a "*European Union*" and now use a single currency called the "*Euro*". Canada, Mexico and the USofA have already got "NAFTA" (the North American Free Trade Agreement) and I'm certain that everyone has their opinions on whether *that* agreement has helped or hurt our USofA. So what's so far fetched? But is it true?

Why on earth would our U.S. President sign such an agreement? Does someone have '*centralization*' in mind? Note that this is the same U.S. President who created the brand new "*Department of Education*" at the national level. Could our U.S. Constitution survive a merge with Canada and Mexico? Would our own lives remain the same, or improve, under such an arrangement?

But again, I want to point out that I am *not against* government. To repeat what I told the high school government class so many years ago:
"government is better when it is closer to the people and...government should only be doing those things that it was commissioned to do."

Let me speak now about where I have chosen to buy a home. The entire neighborhood is made up of "*site condos*". What that really means is that we all join an association, pay minimal annual dues, but the association retains the right to '*control*' what is done on the property of all homeowners. We can't have buildings that are detached from the main house; we can't park vehicles in the open with business advertisements on them; we can't leave trailers or RVs out in the open, nor garbage cans; if our grass gets too long then the association will have it cut and bill us for the favor; if our house is in bad need of paint then the association will have it painted and send us the bill; etc.

There are now some 350 homes in the neighborhood, with a big lake in the middle, and three other lakes around the peripheries, with '*common*' beaches, boat launches, parks, etc. The neighborhood has survived successfully for over fifty years and bigger and better homes are added every year.

This all may sound like there are onerous restrictions infringing on my ability to be '*free*', but I have chosen to live here. Everyone is friendly, kind and helpful, all of us realizing that we're in this together; that if property values go down because of eyesores or soreheads then they go down for all of us. And by the way, I've never seen any home owner actually get his arm twisted in order for him to keep up his own place; we just all kind of automatically do so for our own individual and mutual benefit.

What we have here is our own form of government, one that is very responsive, very close to home, very involved with each other, each of us an active participant in our own community. We accept our own government, and we can vote to change our bylaws.

But if these same '*rules*' were written at the '*township*' level, or the '*county*' level, then I wouldn't like the rules nearly as much. There are some who will not want to pay the annual dues, some who really want an additional detached garage or a garden shed out back, some who need to park their '*work*' vehicles in their own driveways, and those folks can *choose* to *not live* in our neighborhood. But if they would somehow be expected to move completely out of the *township*, or completely out of the *county*, to escape the same restrictions if those restrictions had been written and implemented at a more '*centralized*' level (such as the '*township*' level or the '*county*' level) then the restrictions may indeed be getting too cumbersome, and perhaps out-of-control.

So bottom line, there are advantages and disadvantages to '*centralization*' (and '*consolidation*') but '*freedom*', and more specifically '*freedom of choice*' is best served via '*de-centralization*'. Our Founding Fathers understood this and provided us the tools in order to *achieve* the most freedom possible. And it is *up to us* to protect and preserve that freedom.

Chapter 6

Which Rules Should Exist?

We've viewed '*government*' from several different angles, from the behavior of individuals in society, the behavior of political leaders and politicians, how centralization compares to de-centralization, and even whether *we need* a government at all.

In the end, one of the main ingredients of '*government*' is all the '*rules*' that we are expected to live by.

These '*rules*' may be simple '*restrictions*' as I described that we have in my neighborhood. But they are also called '*ordinance*', '*statute*', '*regulation*', '*law*' or whatever '*category*' that they might be dumped into when they are implemented by some government official or bureaucrat. They are (what most of us believe are) the '*rules*'.

We began our discussions with a review of why different folks would want different '*rules*', whether facts and logic were used to compose the '*rules*', whether someone chose a reactionary feel good measure or whether someone had an ulterior motive.

But the *real* issue that we *really must address* is how to determine *which* '*rules*' should be *our* '*rules*'. Only then can we take the next steps to make sure that our government is doing what we *want* it to do.

A government bureaucrat may want different '*rules*' than other people want because they are most likely seeking job security along with their guaranteed pay increases and mucho benefits. An elected official may prefer those '*rules*' that provide him with an ever increasing amount of power over others as well as a method for providing favors to his election contributors. But the rest of us, the tax paying grunts who are not taking handouts from the government, may quite likely prefer a much *different* set of '*rules*'. And it is the duty of we grunts to make it very clear to the government bureaucrats and elected officials that it is *our* opinion that must be adhered to, *not just their own* opinions.

Our Founding Fathers had their own ideas about our '*rules*', or more specifically and from the opposite direction, about which *crimes* were the type of *crime* that required legislation be written at the centralized federal level. If you review the U.S. Constitution:

"Article. I. Section. 8. ...To provide for the Punishment of counterfeiting the Securities and current Coin of the United

States;..."

"Article. I. Section. 8. ...To define and punish Piracies and Felonies committed on the high Seas..."

"Article. III. Section. 3. ...The Congress shall have power to declare the Punishment of Treason..."

Go ahead and read our '*rulebook*'. I can find *only three* crimes addressed in the U.S. Constitution. Is *that* anywhere near the number of crimes that are considered federal crimes today?

I have also included in Appendix 4 a paper that I wrote as part of my campaign literature back when I ran for State government. It includes another overview of our '*rules*' and is a solid supplement to this discussion. You might stop and read it now to help you see this issue from additional directions.

Before deciding *which 'rules'* should be *our 'rules'* we must *also* decide what type of country we want to live in. But we must be honest with ourselves when we do this. We may need to sit up straight, puff out our chests, take off our blinders and perhaps even tighten our belts.

Do we want our government to be our Mommies? To tell us what is right and wrong and then to dole out our punishment when we have disobeyed or misbehaved?

Do we want to be a socialist country where the government *attempts* to provide assistance for our every sniffle? And I emphasize the word '*attempt*' because socialism is nothing more than communism '*lite*' and it's been proven that communism doesn't work.

Do we want a democracy where stronger groups can override the rights of less powerful groups? Where we all spend our lives playing a game of '*Family Feud*', clapping when we like what the '*survey says*' and simultaneously yelling out '*good answer, good answer*'.

Do we want a government whose philosophy is so non-descript that our politicians can write any law they choose in order to enable their buddies to benefit greatly financially, knowing that some of that money will either directly or indirectly trickle on over to the politicians themselves?

Or perhaps we want what our Founding Fathers *supposedly* had envisioned, that reason that so many of our ancestors came to this land, the concept for which so many have fought and died to preserve, the word that has at times invoked chills throughout our bodies when we heard it sung in our patriotic songs? What about '*freedom*'?

The Declaration of Independence states very clearly what our Founding Fathers thought about '*freedom*' (although they used the word '*liberty*' as opposed to '*freedom*'). It is one of the most basic of all human desires and one that should be obvious (self-evident) to everyone.

> "WE hold these Truths to be self-evident, that all Men are created equal, that they are endowed by their Creator with certain unalienable Rights, that among these are Life, Liberty, and the Pursuit of Happiness – That to secure these Rights, Governments are instituted among Men..."

And then after identifying the most basic rights, they declared that *the reason for government* was to guarantee (secure) these unalienable rights.

Think about today's government. Do we ever hear a current political leader speaking in these grand terms, speaking about '*freedom*' and that the *key role* of our government is to *guarantee* that '*freedom*'? Actually, on the rare occasion when we *do*, many of us quickly shoo the thoughts away as they are really nothing more than unachievable goals, pipe dreams, lofty words from some bygone era, or '*maybe someday*' emotionally charged impossibilities. We bring ourselves back to reality and to thoughts of our daily grinds. We can't afford to drift off into some fairy tale.

Others of us keep our thoughts superficial and pretend that indeed we live in a '*free*' society, after all, think of all the times that we've *heard it said* that we live in a '*free country*', and think of all the things that people get away with doing. We all may know someone who speeds excessively on the highway but never gets caught. We all may know someone who is doing illicit drugs. We all may know someone who is scamming the system, be it for government handouts, insurance fraud, or maybe as simple as doing personal things while on the clock at work. What the heck, we *must be free* if people are getting away with all these '*things*'.

But there's a big difference with getting away with something, and *being '*free*'. '*Getting away with something*'* implies unacceptable or even criminal activity, and '*crimes*' are against the law. In fact, our entire society is based on fighting crime and following the law. Isn't it?

On the other hand, '*freedom*' should *not* be against the law, but there are so many laws out there that some might wonder if we really are free at all.

Returning to the topic of political leaders speaking out about '*grand*' concepts like '*freedom*', some of us shooing away the thoughts, and some of us making believe that we *are* '*free*'; there's a *third* group who *truly believe*, who *know* that things *can* get fixed. We believe that the only way to stay focused on the effort is to keep the big picture, the ultimate goal, namely '*freedom*', always in the frontal lobe of our minds, always at the tips of our tongues, and with it *there* we can continue eating our elephant one bite at a time.

'*People able to be the best that they can be; a place where people are truly able to pursue life, liberty, and happiness...*' The place is right here, in the USofA, but only if we have the *right laws*.

Think about today's laws. Can you name a few laws that fall into the category of '*Mommy doesn't want us to hurt ourselves*'? How about a few laws that fall into the category of '*Socialists want to make believe that our woes will be lessened if only they are evenly distributed*'? Or maybe a few laws that fall into the category of '*Survey shows that most people want the government to do something about x*'? And how about laws that result from '*Politicians should be allowed to use their power to feather their own nests and the nests of their buddies*'? My guess is that each and every one of the laws that fall into these above four categories *also* fall into another category, one of '*We the government know best! Besides, most people can't handle freedom!*' And I fear that this fifth '*category*' is how far-too-many in our government see their jobs.

In 1831, French judge and writer Alexis de Tocqueville visited the USofA and studied the American experiment for nearly two years. When he returned to France, he wrote a two volume work, *Democracy in America*:

"one of the most definitive studies on the American culture and constitutional system that had been published up to that time".[15]

Tocqueville is still quoted extensively, but the quote that I remember most is the following:

"*America is great because she is good and if America ever ceases to be good, America will cease to be great.*"

I've spent much time discussing particular behaviors that we all must protect ourselves against, in our daily lives. I went on to discuss that we all too often excuse our political leaders when they are '*caught*' being involved in these very same behaviors. I've used the three words '*liars*', '*cheats*' and '*thieves*' to simplify these bad behaviors, and those three words do a pretty good job of summing up the types of people who would ruin our efforts at a civilized society.

However, a *fourth* word should be added to this list, namely '*infringer*'. This word may not sound as *bold* as the other three, but it describes behavior that is just as troublesome and must also be protected against.

'*Infringing*' on someone else is sometimes a bit more difficult to quantify and qualify than those other three bad behaviors, although we often '*feel*' it when it happens to us. The feeling it conjures up is a completely natural and predictable one of discomfort, annoyance, or even aggravation. '*Infringing*' may be as simple as a stranger standing too close to me and '*invading my space*'. Indeed it makes me uncomfortable, so much so that my first and immediate inclination is to somehow *regain* my space cushion. But many people are themselves too polite to make a fuss over the poor manners of some stranger who they'll probably never even see again anyways.

But what if that stranger smells real badly? Wouldn't his invasion of your space be all that more annoying? And what if one of the bad smells is the smoke from a cheap cigar drafting straight into your face? Has his lack of manners started to aggravate you yet?

What if it's a hot summer's day and he leans his bare sweaty arm against your own bare arm? What if his lean is more like a bump and you are sent mildly off balance such that you must reposition your stance to keep from falling over? What if the result of your repositioning allows him to cut in front of you in the line in which you were queued? And what if he gets the last pair of tickets available because he now was ahead of you in that line? And what if, after everything else that has happened, he senses that you are steaming and he verbally addresses you with vile and filthy language, perhaps even suggesting that you '*Go F yourself*'?

At exactly which point has this guy crossed the line? Exactly when did he start to infringe? When, if ever, should you finally have stood up for yourself? Exactly when would you have finally had enough?

I'd like to think that I would have responded when the guy first invaded '*my space*'. And if I had this guy with no manners would probably have responded with the '*Go F yourself*' comment much earlier than waiting until the end of my long drawn out scenario described immediately above; but even so I would at least have eliminated him from '*my space*', I would have gotten that last pair of tickets, and I wouldn't have to disinfect my bare arm, either.

The above story about '*infringing*' is really not very earth shattering. However, it does show how minor '*infringements*' can build one atop another, slowly, a little at a time, until you realize, maybe after its too late, that the '*infringement*' has finally gone too far.

That is exactly how our government has worked over many, many decades, chipping away at our freedoms, slowly, a little at a time. It all started before most of us were born but it continues today, a little at a time.

Indeed I am making a comparison between our current government and the smelly schmuck in the story above. *'Infringers'* can exist everywhere.

To recall a quote from earlier in this chapter:
"…all Men are created equal … endowed …with certain unalienable Rights … Life, Liberty, and the Pursuit of Happiness … to secure these Rights, Governments are instituted …"

Anyone who gets in my way in my quest for *"Life, Liberty, and the Pursuit of Happiness"* are indeed *'infringers'* and the government that we have instituted has been charged with the responsibility for helping to protect me from those *'infringers'*.

However, to quote a phrase that I've heard many times: *"My* Rights end where *your* nose begins" I cannot just go and do anything that I want to do in *my* quest because I could end up *'infringing'* on *someone else's* Rights. Thus great care must be taken when defining exactly where people's noses begin, or to state it from the opposite direction, to define exactly where *'infringement'* begins.

In the Amendments to our *'rulebook'* one phrase is repeated that is very similar to a portion of the quote that I've now used thrice in this chapter.

"Amendment V. No person shall be … deprived of life, liberty, or property, without due process of law…"
"Amendment XIV. … No State shall make or enforce any law which shall … deprive any person of life, liberty, or property, without due process of law…"

Life, Liberty, *or property…* Not just *"Life, Liberty, and the Pursuit of Happiness"*. I believe it appropriate in our discussion to compose and utilize a phrase that includes all *four* of these items; thus *'Life, Liberty, Property, and the Pursuit of Happiness'*. And I believe that foursome adequately describes those parts of *'me'* that I most emphatically must protect, and that if anyone should *'infringe'* on any of these foursome that our government has a responsibility to assist in my protection.

Then there's that *other* foursome *'Liars, Cheats, Thieves and Infringers'* that do a pretty good job of defining who and what I must be protected *from*. However, there's another word, and its opposite word, that more completely categorize good and bad behaviors. These two *'bigger'* words have meanings that are a bit vaguer than the above four words that I've been using. They can also mean different things to different people. But for efficiency sake, and in order to broaden our discussion, and so that we can more efficiently refer to those foursome from a positive point of view instead of only from the negative, I will change over to using these '*bigger*' words.

And those '*bigger*' words are '*morality*' and '*immorality*'.

But as I stated above, these words can mean different things to different people. For instance, an animal rights activist will think it '*immoral*' for anyone to eat meat. A fundamental Islamist will think it '*immoral*' for any woman to be seen in public revealing any more than her face and her hands. A southern Baptist will think it '*immoral*' to dance. A global warming alarmist will think it '*immoral*' to drive a gasoline powered vehicle. A communist will think it '*immoral*' to make a profit.

And this list could go on and on infinitum but my goal here is *not* to *define* '*morality*' and '*immorality*'. Instead I intend only to identify the far reaching and divergent views that can be conjured up by the use of these words. Indeed, further and future analysis and definition of '*what is moral*' and '*what is immoral*' will be exceedingly valid and valuable and will forever be discussed and debated. However, for our discussions here, let's limit the meaning of '*immorality*' to those four bad behaviors that I have listed so many times, namely '*lying, cheating, stealing* and *infringing*', and the meaning of '*morality*' to '*not lying, not cheating, not stealing* and *not infringing*'. These limitations will help us focus on the *real* points that I am attempting to make.

'*Morality*' versus '*immorality*'…

How can each of us be protected from the adverse affects of the '*immoral*' behavior of others?

What type of government do we want?

Which '*rules*' should be *our* '*rules*'?

I've now hopped around between several different topics in this chapter, and I've done so for a reason. Identifying which '*rules*' should be *our* '*rules*' is an extremely important question and it is extremely crucial that we get the answers right.

Each '*rule*' that is written will have an impact on we as individuals as well as on our entire society, including *unintended* side effects. So again, it is crucial that we get the answers right.

Many before us have tried to provide us with guidance to help us decide our answers but few of us are equipped to dig through all of history in order to find all that advice much less adapt it to our today's. The best that we can do is to start where we are at right now and then work to change things, a little at a time, moving us into the direction that we choose, again eating our elephant one bite at a time.

To pick our answers we must think things through. To think things through we must first seek out all the facts and then apply our logical analysis. In order to keep our thoughts from becoming so big and complicated that we cannot possibly find our answers we need to keep our questions as simple as possible, to keep them bite-sized. By doing this we will also be able to keep the number of facts that we must accumulate at any one time to a minimum, and thus the necessary logical analysis also to a minimum. With this in mind we have a chance at achieving our goals.

Keeping it simple, before we attempt to identify which '*rules*' we want we must first identify which *types* of '*rules*' that we *want* and which *types* we *don't* want.

In order to populate *these* two lists we must identify our criteria for making our decisions about which *types* of '*rules*' we want and which *types* we *don't* want.

In order to identify our criteria we need to identify what *type* of *government* we *want*. Simultaneously and independently we also need to identify what *type* of government that we are *supposed to have*, and what *type* we *actually have*, and then finally we might compare the *three types* in order to determine how and whether we '*can get there from here*'.

What type of government are we *supposed to have*? As I've stated in previous chapters, to quote the Pledge of Allegiance, a "*republic*", and to quote the U.S. Constitution:

"...every State is guaranteed to have a Republican form of government".

To quote my *Black's Law Dictionary*:

"*republic ... that form of government in which the administration of affairs is open to all the citizens*"

To quote my *Webster's Dictionary*:

"*republic ... any group whose members are regarded as having a certain equality, common aims, etc.*"

Understanding what a '*republic*' is, is crucial to our identifying what type of government that we are *supposed to have*.

To quote one of the best single sources that I have found for explaining what our Founding Fathers had in mind when they first composed our '*rulebook*', a book that I have already quoted in this chapter and in my Appendices, namely *The Making of America*, our Founding Fathers identified two historic types of '*republics*', but weren't satisfied with either and thus invented a *third* type.

"1. the "unitary" republic is one in which all power is vested in the central government. Great Britain is a unitary republic with all power centered in the Parliament.

2. A "confederation of states" republic is one which grants very little power to the central government but reserves nearly all power in the local political units or the states. This is what happened under the American Articles of Confederation, which almost caused the states to lose the Revolutionary War. During the American Civil War, the Southern states also tried to use a "confederacy."
3. A people's "constitutional" republic is sometimes called a "federal" republic or "democratic" republic. This system is based on the supreme will of the people, which is expressed in a written constitution. It was invented by the American Founding Fathers. This American system divides power vertically and horizontally and assigns to each level of government those responsibilities which can be most efficiently and economically administered there. It proved to be the soundest system of government ever devised by man."[16]

"To appreciate the difference between the first and third types, it is significant to note that the British Parliament can pass any law it wishes on any subject. It even passes on the constitutionality of its own laws. Furthermore, it is responsible for the well-being of the entire kingdom, top to bottom. It is therefore called a "unitary republic". The United States, however, operates under the numerous restrictions of the Constitution. No matter what Congress or the states might wish to do, they have to stay within the boundaries of the Constitution. That is why the Founders are credited with the invention of a new kind of republic based on "constitutional supremacy." This makes the "supremacy clause" the cornerstone of the whole American political structure."[17]

And in order to quickly explain what is referred to above as the "*supremacy clause*", the U.S. Constitution states:
"Article VI. ...This Constitution, and the Laws of the United States which shall be made Pursuance thereof; and all Treaties made, or which shall be made, under the Authority of the United States, shall be the supreme Law of the Land; and the Judges in every State shall be bound thereby, any Thing in the Constitution or Laws of any State to the Contrary notwithstanding."

Our "*republic*" definitions from the above three different sources begin to describe what type of government that we are *supposed to have*.

We apparently can refer to it as a *"constitutional republic"*, a *"federal republic"*, or a *"democratic republic"*. Whichever phrase we choose to use the most critical ingredient to note is that our *'rulebook'*, the U.S. Constitution, is the supreme law of the land. Thus, adhering to what the U.S. Constitution says is essential (and ignoring it or *'twisting the meaning'* of what it says is at least deceitful and at worst fatal for our USofA).

What type of government do we *actually have*? Without assigning a *'name'* to it, we might more easily identify attributes that have developed over the years.

Our government:

1. ...acts as if it has a huge pot of money at its fingertips with which to reward its allies, to break down barriers with non-friends, or to quiet the restless. So many folks within our country as well as outside our country seek some level of political clout which can help them get their hands on a slice of those financial resources, to retain what they are already getting, or to increase their amount into their futures.

2. ...has become a gargantuan leviathan against which so many individuals must battle in order to protect their own resources from *being taken*. Unfathomable amounts of resources are spent to *hide* resources from the taxman, to look for ways to *'beat the system'*, to influence the *'rules'* in order to reduce their own taxable burden, or to even hide criminal activity because since it is *'against the law'* there are huge payoffs to be gained as long as the criminality can be kept hidden.

3. ... possesses the most sophisticated weaponry and technology that is ready and able to be used against anyone who the government deems its enemy. Few of us can probably even imagine the level of sophistication to which these weaponry and technology have progressed. If any of this sophistication is being used secretly for nefarious reasons then anyone who stands up against what this government does had better think long and hard before doing so.

4. ...declares its concern for all of those people in our society who struggle most to get a foot up. However, all this voiced concern is usually no more than either nice sounding words that are used to guilt the compassionate public into giving up more of their own hard-earned resources, a smoke screen used to camouflage the government's own nefarious shenanigans, or an excuse to grow itself.

5. ...is comprised of and influenced by so many lawyers whose goals are to search out loopholes, to twist the facts, to confuse the

compassionate public, to construct legal fortresses around their own political compatriots and/or to bring their political *foes* down to their knees.

6. …seems to find no value in reviewing the mistakes of the past or in dismantling any bureaucracy that has either failed to meet its supposed original stated purpose or has outlived its usefulness. Instead it is deemed safer to not *'rock the boat'*. Thus, *'piling on more'* seems the only endeavors that are worthy of the effort.

7. …has become so oppressive that people seek to escape it. Some move, along with their businesses, out of the cities and into the suburbs where government hasn't created as strong a stranglehold. Some move from the metropolitan areas out into *'nowhere's-ville'*, again to escape the stranglehold. Some move their money, if not also their businesses and their families, *'offshore'*, or even to a *'third world country'* in a never ending effort to escape the stranglehold.

So there you have it, *my* views on what our government has become. Do I ooze negativity and cynicism? Perhaps it sounds as if I do but I prefer to think of it as having developed distaste.

In voicing this opinion have I inadvertently sabotaged any effort that any of us might make at trying to clean up this mess?

At a glance, perhaps I have.

However, I *know* that more people are *good* people than are conniving, deceitful, immoral parasites, and I also believe that *good* will ultimately triumph over evil. Thus, my spelling out my distaste is really no more than admitting to myself that we have a problem. And as we all have heard so many times before *"the first step in solving a problem is to first admit that indeed there is one"*. Only then can we embark on the journey to eventually and ultimately fix or eliminate the problem.

Before we return to identifying what type of government that *we want to have*, I have faith that *few* people *like* what our government has become today. Without even comparing what *'we have'* versus *'what we're supposed to have'* versus *'what we want'*, I also have faith that *most* people cannot see the forest for the trees, that making a comparison between these three could be nearly impossible. But to help assure ourselves that we are not alone in our need and desire to *'get there from here'*, nor to think that *'things have never been worse'*, let me please quote again from our *Declaration of Independence*:

"WHEN in the course of human Events, it becomes necessary for one People to dissolve the Political Bands which have connected them with another ... Prudence, indeed, will dictate that Governments long established should not be changed for light and transient Causes ... to right themselves by abolishing the Forms to which they are accustomed ... it is their Duty, to throw off such Government, and to provide new Guards for their future Security ..."

When these words were first written the inevitable option available to the '*American*' people in order to right the wrongs was for the American Revolution to occur. But gratefully as a result of that revolution, and thanks to our ancestors, we have been granted a form of government that enables us the tools necessary to right the *current* wrongs without a physical and debilitating militarized '*war*' being waged. Instead, via the use of focused, intelligent, and level heads, working together, we can right this Ship of State.

I believe that our ancestors saw it as inevitable that government would become corrupt and unmanageable. I believe that they also knew that "*freedom is not free*", and that "*the price of freedom is eternal vigilance*". They supplied us with enough tools but those tools must be used and they must be used by numerous numbers of *good* people.

It is indeed time for some vigilance.

What type of government do we *want to have*? How about we step through the seven '*attributes*' that I listed above regarding the government *we have*, discuss them a bit further and then attempt to present the '*issue*' from a positive point of view (*what we want*) as opposed to the negative (what we *don't* want)?

1. We need our government to be as lean as possible and only involved in those things that it was commissioned to be involved with, like '*securing our rights*'. Political clout should not be regarded as a money making tool. Instead, creativity and productivity in the private sector should be what earns people financial rewards. Government should never get so big that it can disregard with immunity its responsibilities for '*securing our rights*' while instead spending too many of our resources on its own pet self-emulating projects or handing out favors to *their* favorites.

    We need our government to be as lean as possible and only be involved in '*securing our rights*'.

2. Our government should not be viewed as our '*enemy*' but instead be '*on our side*'. A level headed person doesn't run or hide from his friends and allies. Instead, he greets them and even embraces them. But when a '*friend*' starts costing us too much, that '*friend*' may stop being a '*friend*' and instead become a burden.

When those who are more creative and more productive end up earning more as a result and are then penalized at a greater rate with higher tax rates, then the incentives for working hard and taking a risk with a private sector money making endeavor diminish.

When an authority figure starts sticking his nose into everything that we do and starts laying on us so many demands that any level headed individual who considers *'taking a risk'* at a private sector money making endeavor is beat down before he can even summons the courage to try for fear of all the repercussions the authority figure may impose, then the authority figure has too much power and is not *'on our side'*. He is instead a grandiose impediment.

When there are too many *'rules'*, and when *'ignorance of the rules is no excuse'*, then the lesser risk taker won't even try. (*I wonder how many* 'world improvements'*have gone untried because facing the leviathan is too formidable to even attempt?*)

We need our tax burden to be as light as possible and for the *'rules'* to be as few as possible. Our government needs to be *'on our side'*, not *'in the way'*, and they absolutely must not remove the incentives for our taking private sector money making risks.

3. I expect our government to have abilities far beyond those of our enemies in order to keep us safe. If our government showed self restraint and a commitment to never functioning beyond our *'rulebook'*, never willing to go beyond its defined limits, then we all might be able to sleep easy. However, it appears that indeed that is *not* how our government functions.

    Our government, with all its sophisticated weaponry and technology, must use that sophistication only to *'secure our rights'*.

4. Being compassionate is a very good thing. Wanting to help those in need is a very good thing. However, taking from one person to give to someone else is not compassionate unless the person doing the giving *offers* what he gives. If he didn't offer it, and it is taken anyway, then that is stealing.

    Government should not be offering one person's resources to another person. Government employees are certainly allowed to be compassionate and give to the needy but *only* when the offering has been taken from *their own personal* coffers, not from someone else's. Each of us has a responsibility to be an adult and earn our way. Making bad decisions or being incompetent does not automatically become someone else's problem just because the government deems it so. Charities and insurance companies abound and government must *not* try to take the place of charities nor insurance companies.

(I confess that I sit here feeling like a callus heartless ogre. I, like you, have been conditioned to believe that if I don't allow the government to take my money so that they can help the 'needy', that I am a callus heartless ogre. But darn it! I'm a very caring, considerate and generous person. And I always have been. But the government and its thievery are changing me, and not for the better. I'm resenting their holier than thou attitudes and the adverse affects that it's having on me!)

Government needs to focus on what it was commissioned to do, namely *'securing our rights'*.

5.   Lawyers; I become speechless. My belly goes topsy-turvy. Who in this world would attempt private sector money making endeavors without a lawyer on retainer? But if lawyers know more about the law than we do then couldn't they just pull a fast one on us as their client and thus negate any of the help for which they were hired? We can't live with lawyers and we can't live without them.

I'm not at all surprised that our government is full of them. Who would want to enter that government hornet's nest without a solid legal background to protect him self, to understand what he's up against, and to maneuver the hallowed halls?

But suing every person and company with deep pockets; and convincing juries to award such inconceivably huge settlements that it's safer for a defendant to settle out of court for an *'undisclosed amount'*... and the lawyers taking such a shamefully large cut for themselves...; or using their law book savvy to *'twist the meaning of our rulebook'*...

Our government should be *'on our side'*, and *that* may mean protecting us from blood sucking lawyers.

(Again, I apologize because I know that there are good lawyers out there. But how does a normal good person find you?)

6.   Our government must stop growing its laws, and stop growing its bureaucracies. Instead, it must *shrink* itself. It could start by digging through old laws, disposing of those that are out of date, disposing of those that were proven to have been inadequate, and disposing of those that step into areas that are not within the realm of *'securing our rights'*.

7.   Our government must stop chasing our businesses out of our cities, states, country. When they target specific businesses or industries with restrictions, regulations and taxes, those businesses have no other choice but to leave, and others will follow.

Self survival is a worthy activity for any organization,

including a government. But when that government only exists by taking from others and its omnipresence squeezes the life blood out of other organizations that it eyes, then the government has gotten way too big and gone way too far.

Our government needs to be '*on our side*' and stick to the job of '*securing our rights*'.

What *we want* our government to be versus what *we don't want* our government to be... As I review the seven discussions above, with regards to what *we want* it to be, I see that I was cornered into a very small number of phrases: '*on our side*', '*as lean as possible*', and '*securing our rights*' were repeated several times. Add to that list '*help me to protect myself from being adversely affected by the immoral behavior of others*' and you've pegged my beliefs. (*I can only hope that I've kept you with me in all these discussions thus far such that you agree with me, so far.*)

I need to return again to our discussion about '*morality*'. Now that we've traversed the '*attributes*' that define what our government has become as well as identified what we'd rather it be, its time to touch lightly on another view of the '*morality*' issue and *how it is* that our government *has become* what its become. Keep in mind the '*morality*' foursome (namely '*not lying, not cheating, not stealing* and *not infringing*') as well as the four unalienable rights identified in our '*rulebook*' (namely '*Life, Liberty, Property, and the Pursuit of Happiness*').

The deeper I analyze and the deeper I think the more I recognize that '*morality*' and '*freedom*' go hand in hand, so much so that I find that the two are inseparable. Along with that recognition I also see how '*immorality*' and '*government control*' are also inseparable.

In the table below I attempt to methodically and efficiently layout my case:

Morality & Freedom	Immorality & Government Control
Folks who live a completely moral lifestyle are not doing things that would infringe on the rights of others	Folks who don't care if they infringe on the rights of others are immoral and immoral people will not care whether they infringe on the rights of others

When no one is infringing on the rights of others there will be no need to look for solutions to the problem of infringement because that problem won't exist	When folks are infringing on the rights of others, those being infringed upon will look for solutions to stop the infringement. A problem exists which must be addressed
When there is no problem to address, no one needs to look to government for solutions	When problems exist, folks too often look to government for solutions
It would not matter what a politician might promise because folks wouldn't need the promised solutions or the politicians themselves. Politicians wouldn't be able to sell their wares. Politicians would have to seek more productive employment elsewhere	Politicians would promise to solve the problems. Folks would embrace those politicians and their solutions. Those government solutions would affect *every*one including the non-infringers, and those solutions themselves would inevitably infringe. The more rampant the immorality, the more it would ooze into all aspects of our lives, and the greater the assurance that the politicians would thrive
Government would not need to grow. Government *'programs'* would not need to be financed. Taxes would remain low. Folks would keep what they earned and spend it as they wish, saving, investing, using it to build a better world, and even to help others	Government would grow. Ever increasing taxes would need to be collected in order to finance its growth. Folks would get to the point where their taxes would be so high that they'd be unable to save, to invest, nor to give to others. More and more people would be unable to survive without government handouts

| The world would see what moral living and freedom can provide; the world would desire the same rewards and strive to follow the same footsteps in order to achieve the same results. Morality and freedom would '*breed*' more of the same. And what little government there would be might more likely be a *moral* government | The country would become a disaster area. Immorality would '*breed*' more of the same. The government grown out of control would be infested with the same immorality. Ever more tyrannical government solutions would be tried, but they too would not work. Immorality would guarantee that. Government would grow so large that there would be no one left to pay for it. Everyone would have to give up. All would be lost |

History has proven that the above progression will occur.

And per the progression described above, a few more truths can be proclaimed. '*Morality*' and '*freedom*' are inseparable; when '*immorality*' exists then '*government control*' will follow. Using structured logic, we can *also* deduct that '*freedom*' cannot survive '*immorality*'. If *we want to benefit* from the *fruits of 'freedom'*, then *we must be 'moral'*.

But beware. The natural first response to guarantee '*morality*' will be to pass laws that outlaw '*immoral*' deeds, or what many refer to as '*legislating morality*'. Don't fall into that trap. Giving government the power to *define* and then *enforce* '*morality*' will inevitably produce a government who can justify performing their own immoral acts '*for the sake of morality*'. For instance is it possible for the government to determine whether folks are following the '*morality*' laws without government '*infringing*' on the privacy of individuals (an '*immoral*' act)? And with '*morality*' being such an essential prerequisite for '*freedom*' (and a civilized society) and with the definition of '*morality*' being so '*open to interpretation*', wouldn't we simply be throwing the door wide open for more government '*rules*' and inevitable '*infringement*'?

There's one more stipulation that I want to make regarding '*morality*' and '*government*'.

"Amendment IV. The right of the people to be secure in their persons, houses, papers, and effects, against unreasonable searches and seizures, shall not be violated, and no Warrants shall issue, but upon probable cause..."

Even our Founding Fathers recognized that each of us has a right to a certain amount of privacy.

Consider the following:

If you are doing something, alone, in your own home, and nothing about the activity is affecting anyone else, then what business is it of *anyone* else? Or if you are with another adult, in the privacy of your own home, and the two of you are both in agreement about engaging in an activity that, again, is affecting no one else, then *whose business is it* other than the two consenting adults?

But what if the activity is considered a *'vice'* (because the government has deemed it *'immoral'*)? Is it *then* okay to send in the *'vice squad'*?

When I was growing up there was a common phrase that I'd heard, namely *'mind your own business'*. That phrase taught me some lessons about both *'moral'* and *'immoral'* behaviors. And regarding the two scenarios mentioned above (with regards to doing things in your own home) I believe that this *'mind your own business'* phrase is appropriate and called for.

There was also another phrase and it was used to describe *those people* who couldn't *'mind their own business'*, and that phrase was *'busy body'*. Everyone learned to avoid the *'busy bodies'* (except of course their gossipy cohorts) because you never knew what information the *'busy body'* might be gathering *about you* that they could then spread to their gossiping friends.

Yes, I apologize again, this time for using the phrase *'busy body'* and thus *'calling names'*. But in this case *I need to* *'call names'* because it's the easiest way to identify this particular bad behavior, an *'infringing'* behavior.

Assuming that even though no one else is being adversely affected by the private activities going on in someone else's home, the *'busy body'* will even still be affected. If the *'busy body'* somehow *finds out* what is going on, then the activity will no longer be private because the *'busy body'* has new ammunition and is not known for his ability to keep his mouth shut thus the *'busy body'* is affected. And if the *'busy body'* does *not* find out what is going on then the *'busy body'* will get all stressed out and will need to improve his information gathering techniques. He *knows* that something is going on next door; he convinces himself that its *not normal* to have quite so many visitors, and he notes that those neighbors even always seem have their *blinds shut*, too. They *must* be hiding something. The *'busy body'* cannot cope with *not knowing* what the heck is going on in there! The *'busy body'* is definitely being affected.

And I apologize for the well being of the *'busy body'* and the fact that he is being *'affected'*, but it's *none of his business!* And his being affected is self-imposed because of the affliction of his own nosiness.

When government passes laws with regards to '*immoral*' activities then '*busy bodies*' become valuable to have around. We've discussed several chapters ago that our country *needs* '*good people*' to report criminal activity, because our civilized society depends on it. But if the *wrong kinds* of laws become laws then '*busy bodies*' would somehow get wedged into that '*good people*' category and '*busy bodies*' are '*infringers*' and '*infringers*' are *anything but* '*good*' and '*infringers*' should *not be rewarded* with any kind of positive acknowledgement. That same ole' idiosyncratic human dilemma of contradictory inputs, in this case as to whether reporting criminal activity is right or wrong, again presents itself.

There will seem for some folks to be a fine line between '*good people*' who are trying to help our USofA function as a civilized society versus '*busy bodies*' who are *not* '*minding their own business*'. To other folks, no line of any thickness exists between the two believing that this is simply one of those contradictory sets of facts that we as humans take in but cannot mentally resolve. However, there *is a difference*; its just that as with other issues when government gets involved (such as with defining morality), things get very muddy.

Another '*morality*' versus '*government control*' issue that points at government hypocrisy and '*they want it both ways*' is a well known '*vice*'.

'*Gambling*' is an activity that has for a long time been considered a '*vice*' because it's been defined as '*immoral*'. It has for a long time been highly controlled by State and local governments. Many decades ago there was not a lot of '*legal*' gambling allowed. Horse racing was allowed here and there, religious organizations would occasionally have their Bingo nights, and of course there was that one big exception to all those strict controls, '*Sin City*' itself, namely Las Vegas. Over the more recent decades government control of '*gaming*' has not let up, the high tax on gambling institutions and winnings has increased, the expansion of '*gaming*' has been extensive, and a few other changes have occurred.

One of the most notable changes is that many State governments have adopted the almost exclusive ability to profit from certain types of gambling by conducting State sponsored *lotteries*.

In my State of Michigan the American Indian '*nations*' have found a way to skirt the State laws against gambling by erecting gaming casinos on their own sovereign Indian reservation land. Our State government, with its inability to govern over these sovereign areas became frustrated with watching all the money escaping their clutches. So if you can't beat 'em, join 'em; and thus our State, like so many others, chose to cash in on this *'immoral'* activity by getting into the business themselves. Gambling is *'immoral'*, otherwise how does the government justify laws against it? Gambling is deemed *'bad'* by the almighty government and thus people must be restricted from indulging in it *except* when the government can make big money from it. Big almighty government will permit people to participate in this *'vice'*, this *'sin'*, only as long as the government oversees it, regulates it, and cashes in on it.

And then government makes the discussion of State sponsored *'gambling'* a taboo topic of discussion by tying its takings to the financing of public schools and naturally once again the situation becomes exceedingly messy. They adopt the stance that *'gambling is immoral'* but we the government will be patient with all you people who cannot contain all your *'immoral'* urges and allow it *'for the sake of the children'* and thus the funding of our public school educational system.

So here we have an *'immoral'* activity and who is there to jump in, join in, and cash in? Government; their hypocrisy and their holier-than-thou superior attitudes are disgusting.

And of course there are other *'sin'* situations. Alcohol is a *'sin'*. Tobacco is a *'sin'*. Government *must* plunge in and regulate heavily so that they can cash in heavily. Another *'sin'*? Another *'vice'*? You can be darned sure that the government is first in line to benefit financially. After all, those little people just cannot control their urges ...

But hey, wait. Didn't one of the things that we were talking about just a few pages ago have something do with *'infringing'* on the *'Pursuit of Happiness'*?

The government cashing in on *'immoral'* behavior... Hmm... It makes me think... Isn't that pretty much from where the Mob, the Mafia, Organized Crime gangs obtain their power and riches? From taking what is defined by our government as *'immoral'* and capitalizing on it? Building a whole network of *'enforcers'* who monitor the *'immoral'* business being conducted in their own communities, *'taxing'* the profits, demanding *'extortion'* payments and a cut of the action, intimidating their constituents to behave as their *'leaders'* expect? And then to do *whatever it takes* to maintain their power including making sure that none of the *'opposing'* parties are able to acquire any of that same power, including any *'party'* who wants to *put an end* to all of the shenanigans?

Before we dive into one last topic about another *'immoral'* and thus *'illegal'* matter, I'd like to take a quick moment to spin 180 degrees an impression that I've given you thus far in this book. You have by now found me repeatedly ridiculing '*liberals*' and what I've referred to as their contradictory oxymoronic corruption-inducing predicament. (At this point in this book I might also call their belief system '*immoral*'.) However, I'm not about to let conservatives completely off the hook, either. '*Legislating morality*' is where many folks who consider them selves to be '*conservative*' fall flat. Some are like '*liberals*' in that they seem to believe that '*the masses*' need to be controlled but in this case that government must reign in people's vices. This belief is so *anti-freedom* that I can almost understand *why liberals so adamantly avoid conservative viewpoints*. Thus I believe it important to differentiate between '*freedom loving conservatives*' versus '*conservatives*' with the former being the folks who most emphatically protect the concept defined by our U.S. Constitution, the concept known as the USofA.

Thus finally that last '*immoral*' *thus* '*illegal*' matter that gnaws at me, one that can cause even *more* gasps than the topics discussed over the past several pages including the topic that made me feel like a '*callus heartless ogre*'. This *next* topic is one that throws-for-a-loop even the most freedom loving individuals in our country. But I have to talk about it because it hits on so many of the topics we've discussed up to this point. Please let me introduce the topic by asking a question.

Why are illegal drugs illegal (at the federal level) when it required a Constitutional Amendment to outlaw alcohol (and eventually another Amendment to cancel the previous Amendment)? If earlier versions of our State and federal governments believed it necessary to change the U.S. Constitution in order for the federal government to have the legal authority to make a particular substance illegal, namely alcohol, then why didn't it require the same process in order to have the same legal authority to outlaw drugs?

Now don't get me wrong about drugs. I want *nothing* to do with them nor do I want anyone that I know to be involved with them. In fact, I even argue with my doctors when they try to prescribe me *prescription* drugs hoping for more '*natural*' remedies. (But that's just me.)

I see numerous reasons for both keeping drugs illegal and for them to *not* be illegal and we'll address some of those reasons in a moment. However, right now I want to point out that the *illegality* with no corresponding justification in the U.S. Constitution nor its Amendments flies in the face of the whole concept of '*freedom*' and puts into question whether the government has again overstepped their authority.

Could the reason that the U.S. government didn't change the U.S. Constitution to make drugs illegal be because the U.S. government decided to call it a '*war on drugs*'? Does '*war*' somehow mean that the U.S. government does not need the approval of the States in order to have the legal authority to outlaw the substances? As discussed in Chapter 4, does '*war*' make it somehow different and thus gives the U.S. government all the justifications that it needs for '*legislating morality*' and for '*infringing*' on what consenting adults do in the privacy of their own homes when they're not affecting anyone else? If we review a specific excerpt from the U.S. Constitution:

> "Amendment V. No person shall be held to answer for a capital, or otherwise infamous crime, unless on a presentment or indictment of a Grand Jury, except in cases arising in the land or naval forces, or in the Militia, when in actual service in time of War or public danger..."

And then if we pick through those words

> "Amendment V. No person shall be held to answer for a capital, or otherwise infamous crime ... except ... in time of War or public danger..."

There I see a phrase that could be twisted in its meaning to give someone in our U.S. government who is *carefully conniving and cleverly devious* a justification for this '*infringement*'. Otherwise, I see nothing that could be construed as a '*legal*' justification.

The '*war on drugs*' is a very scary topic. The robberies, the murders, the gang wars, the ruination of so many lives, and on the other hand the huge bureaucratic agencies and the immense costs involved with battling this scourge, all would evaporate if those drugs were no longer '*illegal*'. However, the audacity with which many people respond when the topic is even suggested as a topic of discussion only seems to show that many people really haven't caught on to the whole '*freedom*' concept, and apparently they *don't really want 'freedom'* after all. Otherwise, they'd at least be able to discuss the topic intellectually...

One last comment about the '*war on drugs*'. Since those drugs *are illegal* there is big money to be made so the incentives are large for people to involve themselves in the sale and distribution of illicit drugs. And there have been numerous books written that even suggest that very important movers and shakers of the political world are amongst those involved in these sales and distribution activities. For example, a particular book that went a long way to convince me of the need to discuss the credibility of such claims is titled '*COMPROMISED: CLINTON, BUSH AND THE CIA*', published in 1994 and written by Terry Reed and John Cummings. The story recorded via that book includes how Bill Clinton (while Governor of the State of Arkansas), by insinuation George H.W. Bush (while head of the CIA and then V.P. under Reagan), and the CIA were teamed up to import, distribute, and then keep large profits from the sale of illegal drugs. One of its authors and a main character in the book who describes himself as a former contract CIA pilot who was witness to all these things, autographed my copy of the book after I attended one of his presentations. He wrote '*Form a third party!*' above his autograph. As I reconsider those four small words, he sure was saying a mouthful.

(*Have we here another book whose author 30 years down the road will suddenly declare it to be a hoax? I seriously wonder who would go through all that it requires to write a book only to pull a hoax. And who ultimately would be the one who was trying to* 'fool da people'?)

Have you yet gotten your arms around what occurs when the government outlaws '*immoral*' behavior?

We need to be '*moral*' in order for *freedom* to survive. But we need to keep our government '*moral*', too. As with the '*war on drugs*' it is the *lying, cheating, stealing* and *infringing* that we need our government to address, not the drugs themselves. Again, it's that '*immoral*' *foursome* that we have discussed so extensively that people need to be protected from. And '*freedom*' may well be the best answer for solving the adverse affects of the '*war on drugs*', '*freedom*' in this case being the condition of drugs *not being illegal.*

I spoke earlier about running for State Rep on the Libertarian Party ticket. I happened to be in the middle of that campaign when Terry Reed autographed my copy of his book with that "*Form a third party*" comment. At the time he and I were seeing eye-to-eye about the trustworthiness of dependability of the two existing major political parties ...

Note also that one of the largest impediments to folks taking the Libertarian Party seriously is the very topic discussed above, namely illegal drugs no longer being illegal ...

Indeed *government* '*infringes*' on our rights. '*Infringing*' is '*immoral*'. Do we really want our government to be allowed to act '*immorally*'? Because once the '*immorality*' begins it can only become thicker and more pervasive and then the lines that we draw for our government will inevitably become blurred *even more* than they already are and possibly even disappear completely. The U.S. Constitution would become meaningless, '*freedom*' would become unattainable, and so would our '*civilized society*'.

My personal belief is that what is done in the privacy of one's own home between consenting adults and is not affecting anyone else is no on else's business, especially not the government's business.

I also believe that *'immorality'*, when it affects someone else, indeed must be guarded against. But I don't mean when it *bothers* a *'busy body'*; I mean when it adversely affects someone else either physically, financially or legally.

'Morality' is critical to our *'freedom'* and to our USofA. But again I state that *it must not be defined and enforced by our government.* However, what *can* be legislated is when someone else's *'immoral'* behavior adversely affects another person's *Life, Liberty, Property* or *Pursuit of Happiness. That* is when our government should spring into action.

We in this USofA can be the greatest as long as we are *'moral'*, but if we cease to be *'moral'* then we will cease to be great. And we will ultimately cease to be *'free'*. (Kind of sounds like what Alexis de Tocqueville said in the 1830's ...)

Not allowing our government to plunge itself into *'immoral'* behavior *includes* not allowing it to define immorality beyond our *'immoral foursome'*, nor to regulate it, nor tax it, nor cash in on it. *'Morality'* is something that must be *taught* and *practiced*, not legislated. *'Moral'* behavior, not social deviancy, must become what is commonly accepted as the social norm. We all must lead by example and help others to understand the importance of *'morality'* to our *'freedom'* and to our *'civilized society'*.

A fascinating look into our country's history includes an old spelling book that was once the most popular basic textbook of the early 19th century. This book is featured prominently in a historic home that is still on display at Greenfield Village in Dearborn, Michigan, part of The Henry Ford complex (which has for years been declared the most popular tourist attraction in the State of Michigan). The home belonged to Noah Webster, of *Webster's Dictionary* fame. However, the book I am speaking of now is *'The American Spelling Book'*, known also as the *'blue-back speller'* and was first published in 1783 (well over 200 hundred years ago). What is fascinating about the book is that its main components included

"what Webster thought it important to tell young learners about morality ... and the principles of American government".[18]

(Noteworthy individuals of our past recognized the importance of *'morality'* and its inseparable interdependent relationship to the governments of the USofA.)

As the book progresses the word complexity as well as the *'lessons learned'* become increasingly complicated and profound. However, the following four passages are excerpted from the easiest *'one-syllable words'* section of the book and displays the lengths to which Webster went to teach *'morality'* under the premise of teaching spelling and vocabulary.

Some of us may find the passages charming; some may find them hilarious; some may find them ridiculous. Regardless, they make my point:

Do as well as you can, and do no harm.
Mark the man that doth well, and do so too.
Help such as want help, and be kind.
Let your sins past, put you in mind to mend.

I will not walk with bad men; that I may not be cast off with them.
I will love the law and keep it.
I will walk with the just and do good.

A good child will not lie, swear nor steal. He will be good at home, and ask to read his book, when he gets up, he will wash his hands and face clean; he will comb his hair, and make haste to school; he will not play by the way, as bad boys do.

As for those boys and girls that mind not their books, and love not church and school, but play with such as tell tales, tell lies, curse, swear and steal they will come to some bad end, and must be whipt till they mend their ways.

A simpler world, indeed.

Finally, I must address our Founding Fathers one more time. Having studied our history, I believe that our situation today is no '*worse*' than it was in the earlier years of our republic; quite the contrary. Indeed there seems to have been hypocrisy in what our Founding Fathers wrote versus what they did. I don't believe that they believed that all men were created equal; take the whole slavery issue. But it went even further than that. I believe that many of them believed that only the very elite should be in positions of political power and that those who should be allowed to vote needed to be wealthy enough to own a certain amount of property. Many believed that the underclass, regardless of color or race, needed to be manipulated and controlled.

Could it be that they believed that the underclass would be far too likely to base their voting habits on '*feelings*' as opposed to '*intelligent thinking*'? Or that they would behave '*immorally*' versus '*morally*'. And that the elite alone were the best equipped to '*think*' and the best equipped to *define* '*morality*'?

To those beliefs I say that it is *not* an '*elite*' status that determines whether a person can '*think*' and behave '*morally*'. I encounter many, many '*thinking*' and '*moral*' *regular* people and I see far too many of the '*immoral*' type in our '*elite*' politicians and government officials.

Bottom line, I believe that our country is ready, more than ever before, to really knuckle down and work towards this '*freedom*' thing, ready to work together to make things right, ready to throw out the corrupt politicians and to demand that our government start playing by the rules.

So even if our Founding Fathers were indeed hypocrites, they *did* articulate some valuable concepts. They did announce to the whole world via *The Declaration of Independence* their justifications for splitting from Great Britain, and those justifications seem flawless. And they did write a '*rulebook*' that was convincingly thorough, enough so that fifty separate States have each joined into the Union based on the restrictions that would be placed on the central government. Now we must *utilize* that '*rulebook*' for all it is worth, otherwise it will be worthless.

So which rules should exist? I believe that I have made that clear.

At the central government level, laws should be few and restricted to what is *clearly* spelled out in our U.S. Constitution, and not based on a twisted and contorted U.S. Constitution, laws against such things as "counterfeiting the Securities and current Coin of the United States", "Piracies and Felonies committed on the high Seas", "Treason", "war".

All other laws should be left to the States and their subdivisions of local government. Allow those States to function as the laboratories where experiments are conducted, laws are tried then accepted or rejected. And in those local subdivisions of governments, restrict the laws to those that help protect us against the '*immoral foursome*' ('*liars*, *cheats*, *thieves* and *infringers*') with regards to how they affect our '*Life*, *Liberty*, *Property* and *Pursuit of Happiness*'.

And that includes exposing corruption of any in our government and locking up any government official who uses his power as a government official to perpetuate his own '*immoral foursome*' behaviors against any citizen's '*Life*, *Liberty*, *Property* or *Pursuit of Happiness*'!

How can I justify *not* legislating against '*immoral behavior*' that does *not* fall into the '*immoral foursome*'? Because as long as those other behaviors aren't shoved '*in your face*' by those who are participating in them (and instead keeping them behind closed doors) then they are *not* *affecting others*. If they *are* shoved '*in your face*' then they are '*infringing*' on our attempts at a civilized society, on our own '*Pursuit of Happiness*', and possibly on the value of our '*Property*'. Thus the '*in your face*' part of the '*immoral foursome*' is covered by the '*immoral foursome*' and the rights that must be '*secured*'.

Besides, legislating against other '*immoral behavior*' only supplies government with powers that move us further away from '*freedom*' and excuse them for their own '*immoral*' behaviors.

So do you see how this all makes sense? (Has six chapters worth of logical thinking yet proven its value?)

Chapter 7

Which Way Do We Go?

Bumper stickers can be delightful things, especially when they make you chuckle, gasp and think all at the same time. I bought one at a Harley store but can't get myself to actually place it on my vehicle. Instead it hangs in my garage where I can see it everyday. It reads:

"If We Quit Voting WILL THEY ALL GO AWAY?"

This is one that gets my juices flowing.

I believe that it was Benjamin Franklin who when exiting the Constitutional Convention having just completed the writing of the U.S. Constitution was asked what type of government he had given us. His reply was something like:

"A constitutionally limited republic, if you can keep it."

He knew that the country was embarking on a grand experiment in '*freedom*', one that would require endless effort, but that for the sake of '*freedom*' it was worth every effort.

I don't know who gets the credit for uttering the next two phrases, and I've already stated them both elsewhere in this book, but they are certainly worth repeating.

"*Freedom is not free.*"

"*The price of freedom is eternal vigilance.*"

Indeed, we may have thought that someone else had already fought the war for '*freedom*'. But the truth is that we must battle everyday to keep it alive, and to regain those '*freedom*'s that have already been lost. But these daily battles need not be all consuming if only there were a lot of folks on our side in the battle, and if we clearly understand why we think the things that we think.

Do *you* want '*freedom*'? ... for *your children* and *their children*?

In Chapter 6 of this book I wrote something that deserves repeating:

"...let me please quote again from our *Declaration of Independence*:

"WHEN in the course of human Events, it becomes necessary for one People to dissolve the Political Bands which have connected them with another … Prudence, indeed, will dictate that Governments long established should not be changed for light and transient Causes … to right themselves by abolishing the Forms to which they are accustomed … it is their Duty, to throw off such Government, and to provide new Guards for their future Security …"

"When these words were first written the inevitable option available to the '*American*' people in order to right the wrongs was for the American Revolution to occur. … and thanks to our ancestors, we have been granted a form of government that enables us the tools necessary to right the *current* wrongs … via the use of focused, intelligent, and level heads, working together …"

In 1770, prior to the writing of our U.S. Constitution, Alexander Tyler wrote a book called "Cycle of Democracy". The following paragraph and graphic are reproduced from his book:

"A democracy cannot exist as a permanent form of government. It can only exist until the voters discover that they can vote themselves largess from the public treasury. From that moment on the majority always votes for the candidates promising them the most benefits from the public treasury but the result [is that] the democracy always collapses over a loose fiscal policy always followed by a dictatorship. The average of the world's great civilizations before they decline has been two hundred years. These nations have progressed in the sequence…

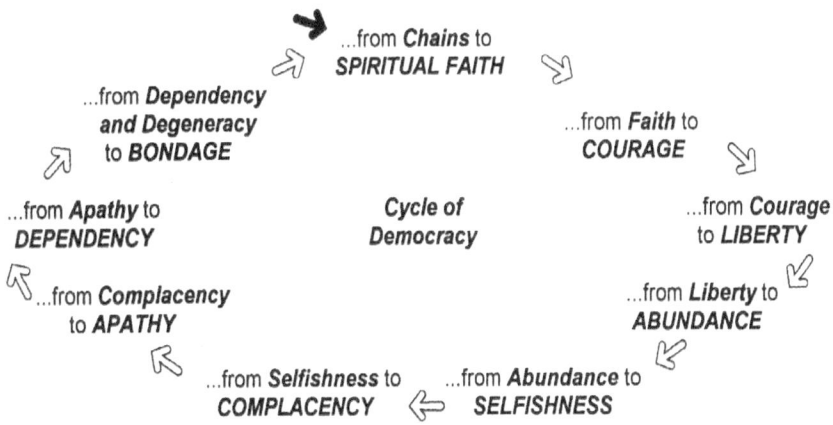

We all fit somewhere in the above cycle. I fear that far too many are locked into the '*Dependency and Degeneracy*' mode.

Indeed we are not a democracy as we've discussed in previous chapters. However, there are certain conditions in our current lives that lean us in that direction. There is one particular political party that claims to do only '*what the people want*'. Is it possible to watch any news program without hearing about what some '*survey says*'? Whereas our U.S. Constitution had U.S. Senators being appointed by each State, the Seventeenth Amendment changed that process such that they are now democratically elected. How many times in our day to day lives have we found ourselves seeking a resolution by '*taking a vote*' and then doing what the majority ruled? Democracy has infiltrated our society.

With regards to the '*Dependency*' portion of the above phrase, in 1995 it was reported by the U.S. government that 50% of all households in the USofA received a check from the government in the amount of at least $20,000. In 2007 it was reported by the U.S. government that the number of households is now 51%. Those checks may be a typical paycheck, a check for contract work, welfare, Social Security, grants, etc. But if *over half* of all households are *getting* a check and they all go out and vote in order to *get more* checks, do you think that we, who *don't get* government checks (and are thus supplying the funds to cover those checks) have *some quick work to do* in order to turn this trend around?

And again with regards to '*Dependency*', how common is it that when there is an issue that needs to be dealt with the first thought in people's minds is that '*the government should do something*'? Whatever happened to self-reliance and do-it-yourself?

And with regards to the '*Degeneracy*' portion of the above phrase, is there any question whether certain parts of our society are becoming increasingly '*immoral*' as exemplified by the vulgarity of TV shows or the publicized behavior of some of our young popular female '*stars*'?

So what's really wrong with democracy? Without repeating any of the references that I have already made *about democracy*, there *is one more* connection that I need to make regarding a *different* topic that we have already discussed but not yet '*tied*' to '*democracy*'.

How do we find *real* solutions that *really work*? We '*think*' utilizing facts and logical analysis. To do this we need individuals who are very well informed on the subject and who know *how* to think. '*Experts*' might even be brought in to help. Then with our very well informed individuals and our '*experts*', both of whom are equipped to analyze the situation and propose a solution, we are most likely to find a *real* solution that *really works*.

But if the *'general public'* *'vote'* on the issue it is doubtful that the *'vote'* will go the way that the *'experts'* recommend. The *'general public'* will include the very well informed individuals as well as the *'experts'* but it will also include far more numerous *non-'experts'* and not-so-well-informed individuals. Some of the *non-'experts'* and the not-so-well-informed of the *'general public'* may have learned what the *'experts'* recommend but even with this knowledge they *may not vote* as the *'experts'* recommend.

Why can I be so sure of this? It is quite likely that what the *'experts'* recommend as proposed solutions will be based on *'cold hard facts'* and thus the solutions themselves may likely appear to be *'cold hard'* and *'tough-love'* solutions. These types of solutions are *not* at all *'warm and fuzzy'*. Most *non-'experts'* and not-so-well-informed individuals will prefer to vote for *'warm and fuzzy'* as opposed to *'cold hard'* or *'tough-love'*.

Thus democracy will *not* result in *real* solutions that *really work* but instead it will result in *attempts* at *'warm and fuzzy'*.

But beware also the *'experts'*. We've all seen enough TV trial-by-jury shows or even daytime TV talk shows to know that *'experts'* with a *slanted view*, maybe even a *politically slanted view*, can always be found. In fact *'experts'* are usually selected *because of* their slanted view. So take great care when selecting *your 'experts'*. I'd prefer the completely honest approach of finding an *'expert'* who deals with *'only the facts'* but since we are all human and thus we all have opinions completely *'unbiased'* may be impossible to find. In that case there are a few different options:

1. Go ahead and allow the *'expert'* who leans in the *other* direction, just to *'be fair'* or just to show your willingness to be *'open minded'*, and accept the likelihood that the solution that is ultimately recommended *will be in the wrong direction*, and *also* accept that neither a *'civilized society'* nor *'freedom'* is really all that important in the first place.

2. Play their game their way except insist on the *'expert'* who leans in *your* direction, accepting that the solution that is ultimately recommended may be just as *off course* as the one immediately above, except at least *your side* will have won this particular battle.

3. Come to agreement with your opponent that obviously the issue at stake is one that falls into the *'political'* category and thus obviously must *not be an issue that should be addressed by 'government'*, and then move on to a different issue. (This will *surely* make them mad...)

Another especially important ingredient in our winning our battles is staying optimistic. Keep a stiff upper lip. Keep your chin up. Stay positive. There are numerous ways of saying the same thing and many folks have made a fortune telling people to do these very things.

But it *can be* very disheartening to see battles you are fighting being won by the opposition. But don't let that get you down because as I've said I believe that good will ultimately triumph over evil. And the opposition is *also* counting on the fact that *you too are human* and are thus susceptible, as all humans are, to being beaten down until you finally give up, shut up, and go away. Remember always that the '*liars, cheats, thieves* and *infringers*' have mastered their craft. They will avoid '*good manners*'. They'll attempt to '*win*' at any cost (because they believe that the ends justify the means). They will try to upset you. They will try to make *you* lose *your* cool. They'll *change the topic* when they realize that indeed you know what you're talking about on the '*current*' topic. They'll call names. They'll attack *you* personally. And if for a moment they sense a kink in your armor they'll kick you when you're down.

Never let them think that they're getting the better of you. Stand strong and don't let them see you sweat (even if you are boiling inside). Don't give them the satisfaction of seeing that they are having an affect on you.

Remember, too, that it's *easy* to be pessimistic. It's *easy* to have a negative attitude especially when so much of the news that makes the news is negative in itself. It's probably another one of those human traits, the fact that we allow the negatives to affect us internally and that we '*feel better*' when we vocalize the negatives and '*let it out*'. It requires *strength* to *remain positive*. You can find strength in numbers, or by having at least one strong person nearby who is on your side. Keep a stiff upper lip. Keep your chin up. Stay positive.

While writing this section of this book the daily news and talk radio topic du jour has been about another U.S. politician in a '*sex scandal*', this fellow being accused of soliciting sex in a public restroom. It's been the number one topic of discussion for over a week. The different responses from the many different talking heads reveal a lot to me.

The accused is a Republican (this time). The liberals and Democrats wailed on about the hypocrisy of this Republican. He had already been targeted by a gay group for having voted against an ultra-liberal piece of gay legislation. Their mantra against this Republican revolved around the audacity of his voting *against* a '*gay*' issue while at the same time he was clearly not as clean, pure and non-'*gay*' as he'd *like you to believe*.

But they never condemned the '*actions*' that he was accused of attempting to participate in.

Then there were his fellow Republican politicians and the stodgy conservatives. These folks indeed adopted a holier-than-thou stance and insisted that the accused Republican resign. They did not want a guy '*like him*' in their political party.

But then there were the '*freedom loving conservatives*'. They pointed out that the fellow was innocent until proven guilty, that he was not even accused of *participating* in any '*immoral*' act, only that he might have been moving in that direction, that even according to the taped interrogation between he and the arresting officer that this had been a pathetically poorly executed sting/entrapment operation, and finally they asked why the Republicans were so ready and willing to throw this guy under the bus when nothing had actually happened?

I was pleased that at least this handful of voices had the integrity to at least *try* to discuss the topic intelligently.

Then my high-schooler nephew came home complaining that during his first week back in school after the summer break, that in Advanced Placement Government class the instructor had spent the entire hour discussing this topic, giving exacting details of what was alleged to have occurred, and then finally near the end of the hour asking whether discussions of '*morality*' should have a place in discussions of politics or government.

My nephew feared that the instructor might be some kind of weirdo. I agreed that he should keep his eyes and ears open, that hopefully the instructor wasn't some type of pervert for having focused so much time on this topic and especially for having specified all the sorted details. But then I insisted that indeed '*morality*' and '*government*' are absolutely tightly interrelated. I explained that the entire book that I was writing revolved around this very relationship and that I couldn't possibly give him a single-sentence response as he hoped I would do. And then he admitted that in the classroom discussion it was never revealed which way the *instructor* leaned regarding the topic, either.

With all these discussions, the '*freedom loving conservatives*' came closest to my way of thinking but none of them addressed the exact issues that I've tried to address in this book. '*Moral*' behavior is indeed crucial, especially when it comes to our politicians, but it is a goal to work towards. We are all human thus we all have secret yearnings that go on inside our heads (and indeed inside our trousers) and we thus are '*imperfect*'. Did the guy actually do something '*immoral*'? Or something '*illegal*'? Is it any business of the government's if something was going on between consenting adults that isn't affecting anyone else's '*Life, Liberty, Property* or *Pursuit of Happiness*'? Did a police officer really have any business attempting to entrap a citizen? (Another mess created because government tried to legislate '*morality*'?) But then, *did the politician '*lie*'* about what happened? In *my* book, if he started '*lying*' then *that's really* when the red flags should have gone up, a clear black versus white, right versus wrong, '*moral*' versus '*immoral*' issue. Or was this a '*none of your business*' '*secret*' that would have remained a '*secret*' had the government not intervened?

The above discussion shows the difficulty with addressing '*moral/ immoral behavior*' versus '*government involvement*'. We all want quick and easy solutions. We all want decisions to be clearly understandable. We all generalize, categorize and stereotype in order to more quickly form an opinion so that we can move on to the next issue, or so that we can supply a single-sentence response that will make for a good sound bite.

"He's a Republican in a sex scandal so he's a hypocrite!"

"He's a Republican in a sex scandal so he's got to go!"

But wait! He didn't actually *do* anything. Perhaps everyone is jumping the gun? Back up a minute. He was arrested because the police officer, as an employee of government, thought that the guy *might eventually* do something that our law books have deemed to be '*immoral*'. But he hadn't actually *done* anything '*immoral*'. At worst, he was attempting to '*meet*' someone new. Egad. (Even though it somewhat sickens me to say the following considering what that politician was accused of doing...) Is it now illegal to '*meet*' someone new depending on where it occurs?

Above there were Republicans and conservatives ready and willing to '*address*' the '*morality*' issue with respect to politicians. Some responded automatically with complete rejection of the culprit while others were actually willing to '*discuss*' it. Either way they at least were attempting to self-police those in politics whom they believe should be held to a higher standard than are '*regular*' people.

On the other hand I heard not a single Democrat or liberal ready to '*discuss*' '*morality*'. As close as they would get was to '*call names*' regarding '*hypocrisy*'. Certainly '*hypocrisy*' is important as it implies a '*lie*' because of '*saying one thing and doing another*'. (But actually I see this particular case *not* as '*hypocrisy*' but instead as falling into the '*none of your business*' category as well as into the '*someone may be trying his best to reach for the '*moral*' goal while admitting, at least to him self, that* *indeed he is an imperfect human'* category, and *that* is honorable.) But still out of the Democrats and liberals no mention of *'morality'*.

In fact Democrats and liberals are usually first to *stand behind* any of *their own* who are accused of *'immoral behavior'* always shrugging it off as *'no big deal'* or *'everybody does it'*. But I believe that it is a *very* big deal, the part about being willing to *'discuss'* *'immoral behavior'*. And the reason that I think that the Democrats and liberals are unwilling to *'discuss'* any *'immoral behavior'* issues is because, as I believe I proved in earlier chapters, the *liberal belief system and agenda are themselves 'immoral'*. After all my years of watching them in action I have come to terms with the following. In the view of Democrats and liberals *'lying'* and *'cheating'* are acceptable as long as you don't get caught; *'stealing'* is acceptable as long as you are the government or depending on who you are stealing *from*; and *'infringing'* is acceptable as long as you do it slowly, inch by inch, a little at a time such that it doesn't bother *too* many *too* much *too* fast.

'Lying, cheating, stealing and *infringing'* is for some reason considered by Democrats and liberals to be acceptable behavior when indulged in by Democrats and liberals *and those behaviors are 'immoral'*.

After all that you've read in this book, if *you* are still finding yourself leaning in a *'liberal'* direction then I have to seriously question *your intentions*. If you think that you are a *'nicer'* person, a *'kinder'* person, a more *'generous'*, *'compassionate'*, and *'understanding'* person and *that's* why you're a liberal, then I will commend you for being *'nicer'*, *'kinder'*, *'generous'*, *'compassionate'*, and *'understanding'* but I'll state in no uncertain terms that you are aligning yourself with the completely wrong political bunch. If you are a Democrat because you despise all of the *'corporate welfare'* that you've heard that the Republicans dish out to all of their buddies in corporate America then I'm with you in despising that fact. But don't think for a minute that the Democrats aren't doing the very same thing. In fact I believe that the Democrats are just as guilty if not guiltier of *that* sin than are the Republicans but the Democrats have just done a far better job of diverting everyone's attention away from them as they are better at pointing fingers and *'calling names'* and more specifically at being *'the pot that is calling the kettle black'*.

(Forgive me for another tangent but this seems like the perfect time to 'complete my thoughts' *about why folks make an automatic association between Republicans and* 'business', *more so than between Democrats and* 'business'. *Most Republicans recognize that* 'financial value' *stems from* 'business'. *They acknowledge that providing products that people want to buy is how value is created. On the other hand, the fuzzy thinking*

of many Democrats causes them to believe that since the government is behind the 'printing' *of currency, and since* 'money' *can be acquired from government, then government must also be an entity that creates* 'financial value'. *The fuzzy thinking comes into play when the Democrats purposely overlook the fact that government only gets its* 'financial value' *by taking it from those who create it.*)

However, if you still lean in the '*liberal*' direction and you do so because you are *really* just having yourself a pity party (because '*freedom's too hard*'), or you are oozing with jealousy (because *others* have *more* than you have), or you think it *unfair* that *others* were '*given*' something that *you weren't* given (and thus those others must be *gotten even with*) then all I have left to say to you is that *you are the reason* that we will ultimately lose *all* of our remaining '*freedoms*' and *you are the reason* that a '*civilized society*' will slip further and further from our grasp, probably never again to even be attempted.

But if instead you understand *just how important* this '*freedom*' thing is then you will keep on reading for additional knowledge about how to battle the '*liberals*' amongst us and inside us.

So what do we do and where do we start?

Good thing you're sitting down.

How about we first examine a little deeper whether *you* might be part of the problem?

But wait. Before we go there let me make it clear that I have no problem with you seeking money from the government in order to accomplish some of the following efforts for finding solutions. After all, I can't think of a better way to spend our money than to use it to *fix* our government. With that being said let's continue.

Are *you* on the government dole? *Are you taking money* from the government and there is question about whether the government should be giving money out for those purposes in the first place? If you are receiving questionable money are you considering whether you should be attempting to extricate yourself from doing so? Admittedly, based on promises that previous versions of our government have made, there are checks being written that *are* justifiable (for the time being). And there are many folks who truly need the helping hand. But if you are one of those people who are simply trying to grab all you can while the gettin' is good and before your particular spicket is turned off, is there anything inside you that invokes a tad bit of guilt for helping to bring your fellow citizens to their knees in order to support this handout heaven?

Well, okay, I better stop myself here. I should have begun this discussion a little bit milder, a little bit gentler. I should have eased us into this drill…

Are you one of those people whose first inclination when there is a problem that needs to be addressed, is to think of the government? Do you first question '*how can we get the government to pay for x*'? Or perhaps your first response is '*there ought to be a law*'?

Or maybe I should move back even a little bit further, back away from such '*large*' and '*all-encompassing*' issues…

So how about…

Do *you* engage in any of the '*immoral foursome*' behaviors? Do you '*lie*', '*cheat*', '*steal*' or '*infringe*'? Don't you think, don't you realize, that we'd all be a lot better off, short term and long term, if *none of us* did these things? Even if you can get away with doing it, don't you see how serious it is to our entire society that we *all* strive for a '*civilized society*' via '*moral behavior*'?

Do you *know* someone who '*cheats*' or '*steals*'? Would you consider trying to persuade them to stop? Or might you rather instead just '*tattle*' on them and '*turn them in*'? You know that sometimes there's even a reward for reporting perpetrators or in some cases it can be reported anonymously.

Do you cuss and swear? Is that really necessary? Is your vocabulary really so lacking that you can't find a better adjective to use in order to make your point? Or are you somehow proud that you have so little class?

Do you have good manners? Do you know what manners are? Do you practice them always even when you would rather not?

Do you spend much time whining about '*woe is me*'? Are you feeling sorry for yourself and thus unable to get your butt up off the couch and do something meaningful?

Do you spend precious time recuperating from the previous evening's drunken stupor or drug induced fog?

Do you waste time watching mindless TV shows or movies or snooping around on the internet seeking a little more titillation?

Do you dump your problems or responsibilities on someone else thinking that even though it's not someone else's problem that if it bothers *them* then they can deal with it themselves?

Do you set a good example for others to see and follow? Are you a neighbor that your neighbors are glad to have as a neighbor? Are the parents of your date happy to hear your voice? Do your own parents ever beam with pride?

These are all samples of questions which we all might consider asking ourselves when trying to determine whether we are helping or hurting our '*civilized society*'. We all play a part.

There's another word that I'd like to revisit. It was one of a few that took center stage in Chapter 1 and then has been utilized countless times throughout the rest of this book. Although I've not hesitated to use it and reuse it, I do recognize that doing so might have caused great discomfort for many. The word can cause sneers and jeers from some, a sickening feeling in some, and seething remarks and filthy looks from many others. And yet I continued to throw this word around, allowing it to seep into our every discussion.

This word for many represents a disgusting group of people, one that most in the mainstream media organizations simply cannot bring themselves to respond to in a positive manner. On a rare occasion those media folks may show a little curiosity, not really understanding why anyone would '*choose*' to be like '*those*' people. However, in many cases little respect is shown and actually contempt, their impatience with '*those people*' having mounted to a point where the media folks and their allies become completely frustrated and ultimately show their disgust.

But it really requires only a little analysis to understand '*those people*' and their '*behaviors*'.

Conservative... *Yikes!* You surely don't want to *know* any of them, do you? You don't want to have to *associate* with them, do you? You definitely don't want to be *called* one of them, and you absolutely don't want to *be* one of them. Or do you?

I know that at least that *seems* to be the popular opinion but does that really make any sense at all?

We've discussed in many round about ways what '*conservatives*' are all about. But maybe we need to bring it all even closer to home.

Is it really unacceptable to believe that it'd be best if a child could grow up in a safe and peaceful household that has both a Mom and a Dad? Of course it's not possible for everyone to achieve but its not an unacceptable goal, is it?

What about only buying what you can actually afford and then paying your bills when they're due? That's not crazy or absurd, is it? In fact, isn't that just responsible behavior, the most basic first step in being able to manage your own finances? Isn't it something that Dad really should teach his young'n's about?

What about '*pitching in*' around the house? Is it really unfair to expect that everyone in the household could do their part to help keep the place clean, tidy, and maintained? And is it really outrageous to expect that your neighbors would do the same at *their* house so that *you* aren't forced to look at someone else's pigsty?

What about doing the homework assignment that you were given? Is it too much to ask for you to put forth some effort and actually try to learn what you're expected to learn?

And what about when it comes to hanging out with family or friends: if you're playing a game is it really any fun if someone keeps cheating? Is it too much to ask that everyone simply follow the rules?

What about when someone always seems to tell lies? Surely if the lie doesn't affect you then you may not really care either way. But if it *does* affect you, like say *you* get blamed for doing something that *the liar* actually did and then *you get in trouble* for it? You don't much want to hang out with that liar ever again, do you?

What if you discover some of your stuff is missing and you *just know* that one of *them* took it. But no one will admit to taking it nor will they give it back. It really hurts when someone does that to you, doesn't it? Don't you hope that it never happens again?

None of these questions seem ridiculous, do they? Don't they actually just sound like normal everyday life around a safe and peaceful household? Aren't these all just simple kinds of lessons that everyone needs to learn and that sooner or later we all hope to be able to live in a household where discomforts no longer occur? That doesn't seem like anyone is asking for too much, does it?

And do you know what? I hate to tell you this but it could very well be that you are being *'conservative'*. Paying your bills, cleaning up after yourself, not dumping your problems on someone else (and maybe even helping someone else from time to time), not lying, not cheating, not stealing... It all sounds like a *'conservative'* lifestyle; it sounds like the kind of household that I want to live in, the kind of friends and family that I want to hang out with, the kind of neighbors that I want nearby.

So if *'conservative'* really seems quite *'normal'* then why all the dirty looks from others when *'that word'* is referred to? Why would anyone want to *deal with* or *do business with* anyone *other than* a conservative? Why would anyone want their government representatives who have the potential to tax and regulate your behavior to be anything *other than* conservative? And why would anyone put any credence in what is being said by those in the media, or their allies, who make it clear that any *'conservative'* points of view are way *'out there'*? Aren't folks who voice that view really just insulting those of us who choose to be responsible adults? It all makes me wonder why anyone would want to admit to any kind of *'liberal'* point of view at all?

The point that I'm trying to make here is that most of us live our private and personal lives as conservative. And being conservative is pretty much the same as being a responsible adult. Why on earth should we not want to surround ourselves with a like minded community?

As I contemplate *'conservative'* the only real *'negative'* that I can conceive are the *'lectures'* that a child receives from the adults around him during all of those years when the *'responsible adult'* lessons were being taught. Could it be that what really makes a liberal a liberal is the fear that he might get another *'lecture'*? Could it be that liberals are so darned wimpy that their entire being revolves around the fear of another *'lecture'*? Good God. This is more frightening that I had originally thought. What could be worse than getting a *'lecture'*?

Being conservative, or being a responsible adult, is a place where most of us live our private and personal lives. But if it doesn't happen to be where *you* currently reside it sure seems like it'd be a desirable dream to have, to hang on to, and to nurture, doesn't it? I'd say it's a goal worth working towards…

So finally, the *big* question:

How can you affect the political process?

How can *you* become active? How can *you* possibly learn where to begin?

1. Vote

"*Get out the vote!*" is one of the most common phrases that you'll hear around election time. They'll declare that *everyone* should vote; that you need to let your voice be heard. They'll claim that if you don't vote then you have no right to complain when you don't get what you want. I disagree with that last claim and with the one about *'everyone should vote'*. But I do agree that voting is important, it's a good place to start, and it is actually the *least* that a person can do.

However, I also believe that if you *don't know what you're doing* or you *don't know who or what you are voting for* then *just stay home and don't* vote! Its *not*, after all, the thinkers who will be staying home and not voting; its *not* the hard workers who are greatly disturbed by all the taxes that are removed from their paychecks who will be avoiding the voting booth; its *not* the movers and shakers, the people who are trying to make a difference and build a better world, who will not be participating.

But it also could be that those who want a bigger cut of the action, bigger checks and more *of* them from the government are also out there voting, too.

Some will say that their one little vote won't make a difference, or why bother because all politicians are the same so it doesn't really matter which one we end up getting. But based on what we've discussed in this book I hope that you can see the fallacy in those claims. No one person including no one politician can fix all this himself. It is *very* important that we stick together in order to *fix* this government and *the more help* that we get *the better*.

So how do we know *who* we should vote for? Now that indeed is another *big* question.

The first '*hint*' that you can get is the candidate's political party affiliation. However, this is only a '*hint*'. Remember that we are all individuals with our own thoughts, beliefs and opinions. As a result no single politician is going to agree 100% with a political party's entire platform. In fact, different individuals in the same political party can have such divergent beliefs that you might wonder how they can both be on the '*same team*'.

There are indeed two major political parties, Republicans and Democrats, but there are also numerous '*third parties*'. The '*third parties*' always form due to frustration with the politicians of the two major parties and their unwillingness to address specific issues to the satisfaction of those who join in with the '*third party*'. Each of these '*third parties*' will have a strong message, one that the two major parties will try to suggest are '*fringe*' issues (which is why they, the major party will claim, have not addressed those issues) and I recommend that you take the time to at least listen to each '*strong message*'. These '*third party*' folks would not be doing what they are doing, going to such extreme lengths as starting a '*third party*', if they weren't extremely committed to their alternative views. In some cases these alternative views may make much sense and not be at all a '*fringe*' issue but instead an issue that the two major parties are simply incapable of addressing or unwilling to address.

But alas a vote for a '*third party*' candidate is pretty much always considered a '*protest*' vote against one or both of the two major parties. When there are *enough of* these '*protest*' votes then the candidates in the other two political parties will sit up and listen, at least temporarily, because it has been proven that plentiful '*protest*' votes can sway the election enough that '*the wrong*' candidate will win the election.

In many cases the major media outlets will not give these '*third party*' candidates much if any attention because they know the impact that a '*third party*' candidate can have, namely '*sabotaging*' the outcome of the election. However, the major media *will* give them attention if they think that the attention could help the candidate whom *they themselves* are teaming for, and '*surveys show*' that the overwhelming majority of employees of the major media organizations, excluding the '*new*' media, do indeed vote Democrat.

Note also that these '*protest*' votes are also usually considered to be '*throw away*' votes. But sometimes it may be worth the '*throw away*' in order to '*protest*'...

Then there are the two major political parties.

Let's first discuss the Democrats. They are by far the most predictable.

Democrat politicians and candidates view and treat their constituencies as victims who need government's '*help*'. Democrats will always promise something '*more*' with an undertone of '*let's get even with the wealthy*'; always.

However, Democrats are also as divergent in their views as any political party could be. What they *do have in common* is that they believe themselves to be the '*downtrodden*' who must stick together in order to make their lives more '*even*' with everyone else. What they also all seem to have in common is their '*woe is me*' syndrome and the Democrat politicians play to that fact.

Republicans on the other hand are made up of those who claim to be '*conservative*', the '*religious right*', and those who are tired of '*big government*'. Some of these groups overlap but not all in each group.

The Republicans also have a lot of folks who prefer the '*status quo*', who would rather '*go along to get along*', and thus there develop large divisions of resentment amongst individuals in this political party. 'RINO' (rhino) Republicans, or '*Republicans In Name Only*' is an often used phrase for identifying the '*go along-ers*' who usually seem to be far more '*liberal*' than they are '*conservative*'.

With these Republican differences rather well-defined due to the well-defined makeup of their voters, infighting amongst members is also predictable, some supposedly being *too* '*conservative*', some *too* '*religious*', some *too* '*anti-government*', and some *too* '*liberal*'. However, infighting amongst Democrats is less obvious and is kept under wraps. Because Democrat voters have far more diverse views, their views are more mutually exclusive, not overlapping like Republican views overlap, *except* that each of the Democrat voters want a '*piece of the pie*'. Ultimately the Democrats will '*work together*' (with each other) with the unspoken agreement being '*if you help me get my piece then I'll help you get yours*'.

As a side note, this '*working together*' makes Democrats believe that they are more '*open minded*' and '*accepting*' of folks who are different from themselves. These folks who are '*working together*' may quite likely *look* different from one another, or live lifestyles that are different from what is most common. Republicans, on the other hand, may tend be more monochromatic and strive to live lifestyles that are more historically traditional. However, thinking that Democrats are '*nicer people*' because of this '*working together*' is a dramatic misnomer. They simply recognize that in a '*democracy*' majority numbers of people are what matters so they need everyone that they can to be on their side (not saying that Republicans don't have the very same need).

In *both* of the major political parties a common basic belief is *also* that *any* candidate from '*my*' party is better than *any* candidate from the '*opposing*' party, even though *that* may be a misnomer, too.

The infighting within the Republicans *also* results in the use of two additional '*phrases*'. One of those '*phrases*' is that the Republican voter will have to '*hold his nose*' when he goes to vote for a Republican candidate who he really doesn't support with the voter's real goal being simply to '*beat the Democrat*'. The result, if the Republican wins, is a Republican who is *supposed to be* representing *you* but who has beliefs that *don't match* your own beliefs. And this predicament is accentuated by the other '*phrase*' which is that '*voting for the lesser of two evils will still result with evil*'; and thus the growth of the '*protest*' vote and many of the '*third party*' candidates.

Another set of folks for whom we must vote are judges. These candidates don't usually come equipped with a declared political party affiliation thus the above discussed '*hint*' is not supplied. The only information that you may be given is whether the judge is an incumbent (currently a judge).

Many of the candidates for the very '*local*' elections will often not have a declared political party affiliation, either. There may be school board members, university regents, dog catcher, etc. without a declared political party affiliation. Every state has different laws thus who gets elected will differ from state to state and between local jurisdictions within a state. This is where your homework will have to begin in order to get your hands on the list of names and positions, before the election, of those who are competing in the next race.

Clearly, more information is needed about *all* of the candidates, whether or not there is a declared political party affiliation. And that's where things become more difficult. Where do you get '*more*' information and how do you evaluate the information that you get? The answers that you can obtain will be based on how much time and energy that you have to dedicate to this task, as well as how much help that you can get for the investigation. But no matter what, beware that all candidates will want to show their '*good*' side, their opponents will want to divulge their '*bad*' side, and seasoned politicians have survived thus far based on their ability to answer, or not answer, important questions.

A most simple thing that you can do, which I have done numerous times, is to simply call the candidate's office, or campaign office, and ask a very short and concise list of questions, listen very carefully to the answers, and then compare the answers of one candidate to the other. Which questions you ask should be very relevant to both you and to the position that the candidate seeks. Discussions later in this chapter should help you develop your questions so we won't focus on your questions right here. But your ability to *ask the right questions* will help you to develop a *better* ability to ask the right questions, so practice, and practice.

Note also that the willingness of the candidate or his staff to actually speak to you can also help to establish just how '*slippery*' this candidate is, and that too is meaningful information.

As I stated above, I've numerous times called candidates and asked them questions. A few examples of *my* questions might help to make my point and to start your own brain calculating...

For State level candidates, being in the State of Michigan, I have a ready made question that folks in few other states can use: "*The State of Michigan is one of only a handful of States that has a full time legislature. Do you think that we should continue the legislature full time, and why?*" Note that I have a couple of thoughts about what would be an acceptable answer, and I've found few candidates whose response even approximates one of my desired answers.

At another time, during a period of severe national anti-Second Amendment sentiment, I picked up on the '*current topic*' and asked: "*What are your views on 'gun rights'?*" Again, I was prepared with my own views before calling the candidates, but I gave them no advanced warning of which way I wanted them to answer.

Finally, when it comes to judges, they may be the most difficult of all. But I have my single question which really gets down to the nitty-gritty, for me, and let's me know whether I want them sitting in judgment of my fellow citizens: "*What are your views on 'jury nullification'?*" (If you've read Appendix 4 then you will know more about what I think about this issue. A '*good*' judge will recognize it and suggest that it has value. A '*bad*' judge will have never heard of it or might even declare it '*illegal*'.)

I trust that you will eventually be able to compose your own questions. And don't be too scared to make the calls. It is the candidates, after all, who are applying for the job of serving *you*, being employed *by* you, and you have every right to a pre-hire interview.

Another major category of election options are '*new laws*'. The fact that you are being given the privilege of voting on these is because they are such important issues that they will require that existing law be changed that extend to founding documents such as a Township or City Charter, a State Constitution, and even the U.S. Constitution. Most times they will be a request for more of your money in order to fund something specific. But many times it will be placing additional restrictions on someone's freedoms. These '*referendum*' or '*initiatives*' are hopefully not written in legalize lawyer-speak, and are self explanatory. But some can be very confusing because, as in the State of Michigan, a '*yes*' vote is required in order to change existing law. Thus you sometimes get verbiage where '*yes*' really means '*no*' and '*no*' really means '*yes*'. For example, in order to make an existing law no longer valid, you'd have to vote '*yes*' that you *don't want* the law. When you start speaking with lots of '*not*'s, '*don't*'s and '*won't*'s instead of the positive '*will*'s and '*shall*'s, the meaning can sound like you are voting for opposite what you are supposed to be voting for. And sometimes it seems that the confusing words are chosen on purpose, just to confuse everyone. So pre-reading the proposed '*new law*' before Election Day is highly recommended.

Another very important event that occasionally comes up at non-regular election times is a '*recall*' vote. There are times when voters believe that a politician has done something so egregious that the only way to '*deal with*' that politician is to *boot him out now*! To do this, after enough petition signatures have been gathered, a special election will be conducted to determine whether the politician is ejected. Note that gathering those signatures on these petitions is a critical step in this process, something that you might '*help*' with. Note also that the threat of '*recall*' has been effective in the past in keeping politicians in line with the desires of his voters, and with cleaning house of bad politicians. Those '*bad*' politicians think that they can get away with contrary votes to the desires of their constituents and depend on the fact that many people will '*forget*' what they did by the time the next '*regular*' election rolls around. This '*recall*' process is another one of the safeguards built into our system that we should utilize when necessary.

Election Day is *one* thing that you can do, and as I said earlier, '*at least*' you can vote. But there are lots more that you could be doing.

2. **Help A Candidate**

You may find a particular candidate that you especially want to support in an upcoming election. You might volunteer to help him, or of course (what they usually *really* want) you could contribute money.

But there's more than just specific candidates at election time, even though *that* is a time when you can get a better bang for your buck because *that* is when the candidates and the voters are listening most intently. All year every year is also a time when your voice could be heard. In fact when a candidate is not quite so consumed with campaigning and after he has won his election and has taken office he may be able to make more time available to listen to his constituents, including you. And in many cases candidates who represent your views but are in a different '*district*' and thus cannot be voted for by you, will still appreciate and benefit from hearing from you.

Also, hearing more than a single voice sending the same message in unison can be more persuasive. As we've hopefully learned from the Democrats, the larger the number of voices then the louder the message. In fact, get-togethers such as '*pep rally*'s of like minded individuals, where all remain '*civil*', can be very effective at building support, motivating others, and increasing the decibel levels of your opinions.

3. **Petition Drives**

The above '*recall*' discussion touches on another topic. In many states '*petition drives*' are a way that voters can get potential '*new laws*' put on the ballot. If the State Legislature won't consider a particular '*new law*' (or a change to an existing law) then the voters can work together via a '*petition drive*' by obtaining enough valid voter signatures to force the '*new law*' onto the ballot for all voters in the State to vote on, bypassing the legislature. Note that signing a petition does not mean that you agree with the proposed '*new law*' but that you agree that the voters should be allowed to vote, on Election Day, on whether it should become a law. And these '*new law*' petitions are another opportunity to help. Again, volunteers will be needed to collect all the required signatures.

4. **Jury Duty**

If you get notified for jury duty, please go, please participate. But when you do, remember the following quote from the Juror's Handbook:

"We recognize, as appellants urge, the undisputed power of the jury to acquit, even if its verdict is contrary to the law as given by the judge, and contrary to the evidence … If the jury feels that the law under which the defendant is accused is unjust, or that exigent circumstances justified the actions of the accused, if for any reason which appeals to their logic or passion, the jury has the power to acquit, and the courts must abide by that decision." U.S. vs. Moylan, 417 F 2nd 1002, 1006 (1969)[19]

Or in other words, '*jury nullification*'.

5. Select An Issue, Get Involved, and Become An Expert

But which issues are the ones that might interest you? Below I will list many '*issues*' that have been debated over the past several decades, very important issues that either need to be protected, fixed, or even reversed. Its not necessary to think of '*new*' issues since there are so many already identified. Also, there are numerous groups and/or organizations that are already formed who are already attempting to inspire government to address their issues. You might want to investigate these groups/organizations to see if any of them suit you, your beliefs and your desires.

In a previous chapter I mentioned '*single issue voters*'. As life proceeds its not long before each of us realizes that we cannot possibly work on fixing '*everything*' that is bothering us. However, picking one or two issues and working on them until it '*gets resolved*' is how many folks have chosen to fight their battles. In fact, '*single issue voters*' have done just that. They've focused their energies on just one issue in hopes that all that focus will help assure '*resolution*'. And its not that they don't care about other issues, too. It's just that they have chosen their one most important issue.

Regretfully, there are times when some '*issues*' simply cannot be '*resolved*' at a certain time in history. A wise person will recognize this predicament and hopefully put their most important issue temporarily on the back burner and change their focus to a different issue. The unresolved first issue need not be forgotten because it is doubtful that it will get fixed while no one is looking. It simply gets moved down the list until '*times are more conducive*'.

So now, how do you go about selecting an issue? Take your pick:

A. Abortion

The single most dependably prominent issue that will be discussed during every regular election where candidates are running for office is *abortion*. The voters who find this the most important issue, whether they support or oppose it, are the most vocal of the '*single issue voters*'. These '*single issue voters*' are often so adamant about this issue that nothing else matters even if it ultimately sabotages an election for an otherwise '*good*' candidate. Remember that no one is going to see exactly eye to eye with you on every issue.

What do I think about abortion? Considering the '*immoral foursome*' and the four Rights that need to be protected, the '*cheating*' a person of their '*Life*', or the '*stealing*' of a person's '*Life*', is about as basic as it gets. It must be protected against and punished when it occurs.

We all know that it is an accepted view that '*the miracle of life*' begins transpiring in the belly of a woman the moment an egg gets fertilized. But for some reason so many in the '*medical community*' as well as '*liberal judges*' have deemed that '*Life*' really doesn't begin until some other '*moment*' that occurs between the second and third trimester of the pregnancy. And thus abortion is not really taking a '*Life*' until after that *other* '*moment*'.

Personally I have great difficulty reasoning that '*the miracle of life*' prior to this *other* '*moment*' is more or less just a cancer-like growth, a parasitic conquistador, an unviable tissue mass; but you must make up your own mind...

B. Guns

The second most dependably prominent issue is the Second Amendment:

> "... the right of the people to keep and bear Arms, shall not be infringed".

What do I think about guns? A person has the first and ultimate responsibility when it comes to protecting his own '*Life, Liberty, Property* and *Pursuit of Happiness*'. A gun in the hands of a '*good*' person who knows how to use the gun can help protect many in our society. Our Founding Fathers recognized this fact and nothing has changed to alleviate this fact.

C. Election Fraud

This issue is perhaps the most '*frightening*' and '*unthinkable*' of all the issues, from *my* point of view. If we are all living according to a certain amount of '*democratic*' decision-making and were that '*democratic*' process to be corrupt then we are all simply keeping ourselves and each other busy with all the '*election talk*' that we indulge in. If the elections are fraudulent then we are all nothing but puppets of some '*secret power*' that are stacking the vote from behind the scenes. Important issue? Indeed.

Go ahead and call your State's Secretary of State. I'm certain that he'll assure you that all is under control. But is it, really?

D. K-12 Public Education

This issue deserves as much attention as any. Without question teaching our children what they need to know as well as '*how to think*' is essential. And I have little faith that these two things are what our educators are doing based on the number of Democrats and liberals that exist today.

First off we must eliminate the brand new U.S. Department of Education before it becomes another stronghold of the U.S. government. My reading of the U.S. Constitution does not allocate that power to the U.S. government (unless you suggest that one of the eleven '*twist its meaning*' items is valid).

Secondly, I believe that we must install '*free market*' types of incentives into the entire educational system so that our children will learn the rules of '*free market capitalism*' as well as make sure that there are motivational reasons for competition amongst our educators to do their best and to do better than the educator next door or down the block. The way that the unions currently function guarantees each teacher to receive the same pay whether they are more successful than their fellow teachers but instead based on length of service. There is no reason for a teacher to '*work harder*' or '*do better*'. In fact the exact opposite occurs. Why bother even doing a '*good*' job when you'll get the same pay either way. And even if your performance is rather poor your job and paycheck will be protected.

'*Vouchers*' are a good idea. It allows different teachers, different schools, and even different districts to compete for the voucher dollars. And I'd allow voucher dollars to be used at private schools, too, with few strings attached. The best teachers, the best schools and the best districts would survive and thrive, inspiring others to improve their skills, and the education provided would more likely keep improving, too.

Note that there are Democrats and liberals who claim that the reason that children aren't learning is because they aren't being placed into schools at a young enough age, that government should *also* be providing preschool for the younger children. The facts are that children learn best when the learning begins at home. Expecting government to do a better job than the family can do in those very young and formative years is absurd. What very young children need is Mom, Dad, siblings and extended family, not some government employee.

And when considering what Mom and Dad can do, take note of all of the home-schooling going on these days, and take note of the performance statistics between home-schooled children and the products of government schools. One fascinating statistic is to note how many home-schooled children enter and win in national spelling bees...

Finally, there needs to be a way to place greater distance between government and our children. I'm not certain how to do this when the money for schools is collected by the government, but I'm certain that if we put our '*best minds*' to work on this problem that they'd come up with a *real* solution that would *really* work.

Undoubtedly helping to educate the children of our community is something worthy of my tax dollars, and I will not complain about that one if it were the only '*general welfare*' item I was asked to '*contribute*' to. However, without '*free market competition*' I don't see how education can possibly succeed.

And, yes, I'd even be willing for my '*contribution*' for voucher dollars to be shared with home-school teachers, too.

E. Social Security

I cannot imagine that there is anyone left in this country that doesn't see the coming train wreck with our Social Security system. Actually, those who won't allow themselves to see it must be blinded, instead, by what they see as an endlessly increasing supply of tax dollars that will need to be harvested from the taxpayer's bank accounts.

I won't attempt to quote any of the estimates that I have heard over the years, but I shutter to think of how much each of the still working citizens will need to cough up in order to support the elderly of the near future with us baby boomers about to retire.

Undoubtedly we all know that Social Security is not like an insurance company or a retirement fund. Money has not been '*set aside*' to be invested and to accumulate. Government writes laws to require businesses such as insurance companies and retirement funds to maintain an ample amount of liquidity (available cash) to protect their customers by protecting the company's own solvency, but they *don't* require the same of themselves. Instead all Social Security '*investments*' have been siphoned off to pay for other U.S. government projects.

But few politicians are gutsy enough to even discuss this issue because that only puts fear into the largest voting block in the country, the seasoned citizens, and those seasoned citizens already have so much to worry about that even *considering* that their Social Security checks may stop arriving each month will be enough to send them over the edge.

F. Veterans

Are there any who deserve our honor and appreciation more than our veterans? Think about what they have done for us. Besides taking relatively low wage jobs that can be extremely dangerous, likely experiencing emotionally traumatic events that could haunt their dreams for years to come, maybe lose body parts, and maybe lose their lives, they have also helped to provide us with a country where we can write and read books like the one you're reading, and where we can act on issues that disturb us with regards to our government.

Our U.S. government does not do enough to support our troops once they arrive back home to reacquaint themselves with life in the USofA, especially when they suffer from combat-caused debilitation. No more a worthy '*issue*' exists than helping our heroes. (Hopefully they can accept our show of gratitude).

G. "War on Drugs"

How do we *really* win this "*war*"?

H. Illegal Immigrants

This issue is *huge*! The ramifications are *huge*! Much of the '*illegal immigrants*' problem gets blamed on our porous border with Mexico. However, that is only *part* of our problem.

I am absolutely in support of '*legal*' immigrants, after all both pairs of *my* grandparents were themselves immigrants to this country, but '*legal*' immigrants. Individuals who are here *illegally* are *criminals*. So why isn't something done to stop them, arrest them, and arrest those who knowingly employee them? Is it somewhere written that it's okay for *certain* people to break *some* laws? Can I pick a handful of laws that *I want to break* and use *those* lawbreakers as a justification? *If they can break a law or two and get away with it, then why can't I?*

Living here in Michigan I thought that I was far away from any '*Mexican border*' problems but now I find them working for neighbors, competing with me for jobs, not speaking English, not paying taxes, and having '*anchor babies*' that will help them become more tightly ingratiated into our USofA, including our welfare systems, our free schools, the guaranteed care in our Emergency Rooms, etc.

And the fact that so many can be living here illegally, how many '*enemies*' of our country are here illegally, too, like terrorists, etc. But wait, aren't people who break our laws *enemies* of our society working against our desire for a '*civilized society*', working against the most basic rules that we live by?

Aren't we supposed to be protected from '*enemies both foreign and domestic*'?

A part of this issue that touches closely to topics being discussed in this book has to do with the fact that *every* immigrant to the USofA comes here from a place with a very different form of government. Only the USofA has *our* form of government. As a result every immigrant will have a different attitude *about* government, different expectations *of* government, and will have developed a different way of *dealing with* the government. Even many of us who were born and raised as American citizens don't have a very good understanding of our own government and that is in fact the very purpose of this book, to bring everyone up to speed. So how can we possibly expect an immigrant to think like we think and value what we value?

Legal immigrants are far *more* likely to be those who are coming here in order to work hard and contribute to our society. They are also required to learn much about our form of government as a prerequisite to becoming citizens.

Illegal immigrants are far *less* likely to live up to any standards or expectations that we place on ourselves or our fellow citizens. After all, the very first thing that every illegal immigrant does is break our laws. The moment that first step is taken onto our soil they are a criminal. Doesn't that equate to being an announcement that they are clearly *not* here to *contribute* but instead to take what they can get while they do whatever they can get away with doing?

Finally, by coming in the back door they are never required to learn what we expect them to learn about our form of government *and* the expectations that we have of ourselves and our fellow citizens. So on top of everything else mentioned above, consider how they might skew an election were they *also* able to scam the privilege of voting, too.

I. English as our Official National Language

While growing up it was common that when visiting with my Mom's siblings and parents that the bunch of them would veer off and speak in the language of the '*old country*'. This would always place the rest of us, including my Dad, at a disadvantage. Clearly what was being discussed was something that was supposed to be kept secret from the rest of us. And the rest of us felt predictably insulted by this behavior, as outcasts.

If ever I enter a place of business and I hear the '*worker*' talking in a non-English language to someone else I turn around and I leave the place. I don't feel welcome, I don't feel safe.

Knowing a second language is indeed commendable and valuable. And to keep it up one must practice. However, when conducting business or communicating with a government representative, open and honest communication is essential in order to trust those with whom you are attempting to converse.

Note that my same '*relatives*' discussed above *also* refused to settle down into the community where so many of the other folks from the '*old country*' had moved, insisting that *their* kids were going to become *Americans* and thus speak fluent English. But they also expected those kids to speak the '*old country*' language at home, as well.

We all know that miscommunication between individuals is a major cause of friction between individuals. We should do our best to communicate effectively, and efficiently. But when you come to the USofA one of the requirements should be that you adapt to the USofA, and that includes *not expecting all of us to change to accommodate you*. Nor should we be expected to cough up the dough for the expense of our government's efforts at accommodating so many other languages.

Is it that I don't care that it's hard to learn a new language? Not at all; but I shouldn't be forced to pay for more shortcomings of other people.

J. IRS

This is a multi-faceted issue.

- Taxes are far too high
- The Tax Code is so complex and convoluted that the more tax experts that you hire to calculate your taxes the more different answers you'll get. Even the IRS admits that the answers that they themselves provide via their own '*help*' line are more often incorrect than not.
- There seems always to be a '*tax protest*' lawsuit going on somewhere in our country where the '*defendant*' is simply requesting that the IRS '*show me the law where it says I must pay and I'll pay*', and some of the '*defendants*' are indeed being found '*not guilty*'.
- All human beings have a Right to earn a living in order to survive (as a sub-condition of the Right to '*Life*') and many believe that it is thus '*immoral*' to deny an individual this Right by taxing the wages paid for work performed by the individual.
- I have been told that the Tax Code defines '*income*' as '*corporate profits*', '*investment income*', and *not* wages paid for work performed by an individual.
- It has been said that the Sixteenth Amendment which installed the U.S. Income Tax was never ratified by a quorum of States and thus it was never legally accepted as an amendment to the U.S. Constitution, and that out of frustration President Roosevelt simply demanded that it be added regardless of the failure to meet the requirements of the

ratification process. Consider the book titled *The Law That Never Was* published by the Constitutional Research Assoc. (1985).

- Another argument against the U.S. Income Tax is based on a purposeful deception that was installed by stealth via the Fourteenth Amendment. Within the first couple of paragraphs of the U.S. Constitution there exists the following phrase:

    "Representatives and direct Taxes shall be apportioned among the several States which may be included within the Union, according to their respective Numbers, which shall be determined by adding to the whole Number of free Persons, including those bound to Service for a Term of Years, and excluding Indians not taxed, three fifths of all other Persons."

The Fourteenth Amendment made this sentence no longer valid and was added following "*The War Between the States*". Note that what this phrase was talking about was that taxes were to be paid to the U.S. government by the States themselves and the amount to be paid would be based on the *population* of each State. Note also that the '*three fifths of all other Persons*' portion of that phrase referred to '*slaves*' and it is absolutely commendable that the 3/5ths insult was eliminated.

However, the Fourteenth Amendment *does not specifically address* the '*direct Taxes*' portion that was *also* dropped. What it *did* do was announce for the first time that all citizens of the separate States would now automatically also be citizens of the '*United States*'. It is argued that the result of this is as follows:

a. Each *State* was to pay taxes to the U.S. government since it was the *State* entities that had actually contracted with the U.S. government via the U.S. Constitution. As a protection against oppressive government, there was never to be any one-to-one relationship between the U.S. government and the individual citizens of the separate States.

b. In order to '*legally*' and '*constitutionally*' force slavery to become illegal due to the power of '*States Rights*' (see the Tenth Amendment) the U.S. government had to make each individual citizen of the separate States *also* citizens of an entity known as the '*United States*' which (elsewhere in the U.S. Constitution) is defined as the District of Columbia (the seat of government) and territories (such as Puerto Rico, Guam, etc.). The U.S. Congress (also elsewhere in the U.S. Constitution) is responsible for all laws in the District of Columbia and *could* legally outlaw '*slavery*' in D.C. Thus, all of *us* suddenly became subservient

132

to any law written by the U.S. Congress.

c. Based on the above condition the '*direct Taxes*' portion of the '*dropped*' phrase was being addressed because D.C. would simply continue to function as the separate States had functioned, namely paying taxes based on population. However, *everyone* was now a citizen of D.C. and thus '*legally*' (even though not physically) part of the population of D.C. and thus *now* the U.S. government could '*legally*' tax *every individual* in the USofA.

Please go ahead and read this IRS section again. If indeed this is what occurred then we all have been snookered in the most deceitful manner. And if indeed this is what occurred then we may need to add this one to the list we used in Chapters 2 and 3 regarding "…. **Methods for Twisting the Meaning of Our Rulebook**".

*   Just think about all the emotional depression that permeates our country around April 15th each year, and the fact that it could be eliminated were the IRS eliminated.

K. State's Rights

The more I study "*The War Between the States*" the more I believe that *that* war was *really* fought over '*State's Rights*'. The southern States that bailed out of the '*union*' did so because they believed that the U.S. government had broken the contract they had signed with the States, namely the U.S. Constitution, by passing unconstitutional laws. (This adds credence to the argument regarding the Fourteenth Amendment discussed in the bullet points immediately above.) These '*Tenth Amendment*' or '*State's Rights*' battles continue today.

L. Eminent Domain Has Become Land/Property Confiscation

It has become far too common for '*local*' governments to *take* land from individuals in order to '*improve*' their local community and then pass the land on to a developer. '*Eminent Domain*' is a concept that exists because there are indeed times when an individual refusing to sell their land to the government would prevent needful things such as the widening of a road. But for local communities to twist that concept such that '*additional tax revenue*' is all the excuse they need as their justification to '*improve*' their local community then the government has gone too far and is out of control.

M. Our 'Money' and the Federal Reserve System

This is another complicated issue but so incredibly important. The U.S. Constitution states:

> "Article. I. Section. 8. The Congress shall have Power ... To borrow Money on the credit of the United States; To coin Money, regulate the Value thereof, and of foreign Coin, and fix the Standard of Weights and Measures; To provide for the Punishment of counterfeiting the Securities and current Coin of the United States ..."
>
> "Article. I. Section. 10. No State shall ... make any Thing but gold and silver Coin a Tender in payment of Debts ..."

Our '*money*' is no longer based on gold and silver. Instead it is all based on I.O.U.s to be paid back to the private company called the Federal Reserve System. This all started when our country went bankrupt back in the early 1900's and President Roosevelt needed a way to finance his U.S. government and their existing and '*new*' endeavors. The Federal Reserve System is owned by a group of international bankers who wanted a guarantee that the U.S. government would cover any '*bad loans*' that their other banks might make. Thus a deal was struck between the U.S. government and the private Federal Reserve System bank. Note that President Roosevelt used all of the private property of individuals throughout the USofA as the collateral to guarantee repayment of the loans that the U.S. government would take.

As I stated above, our '*money*' is no longer based on gold or silver, but is instead based on I.O.U.s. The following little story is told to explain why this situation is so hideous:

> Let's say that you go to the bank and take out a loan for $100, and let's say that the bank will charge you $10 interest for the use of their money. Thus, in the end, you will be required to pay the bank both the $100 and the $10 for a total of $110.

> But all of our money is based on I.O.U.s, or debt, or in other words on loans taken from banks, and so a problem occurs. That extra $10 to cover the interest on your loan has to come from somewhere otherwise it cannot be paid back to the bank, and the only place it can come from nowadays is from a different loan from a bank. Thus, in order for you to pay back that extra $10 you must get that $10 from somebody else who took out a loan, for say $100. But now that guy only has $90 and he still needs to pay back his own loan for $100 plus its interest of $10. He is thus $20 short, which he'll have to get from somebody else's loan ...

> And so on, and so on ...

Do you see how quickly our entire society is thrown into a never ending spiral digging ourselves deeper and deeper with someone inevitably *having to* declare bankruptcy and lose everything? Our government *forces* this to happen because our money is no longer based on gold and silver.

The above is just the tip of the iceberg because when you start to understand where our tax dollars actually go, how '*inflation*' is controlled in order to keep us from '*catching on*' to the above scam while making sure that most of us are '*financially broke*' by retirement age and to give our U.S. government a bottomless pit of money to spend (with our personal belongings as collateral) you can begin to realize how vulnerable we are to any other country who '*buys our debt*' …

A book that you might read is *The Creature From Jekyll Island*, published by American Opinion Publishing, Inc. (1994). It starts out like a mysterious spy novel …

N. U.S. Sovereignty

In Appendix 3 I discuss State borders versus how the U.S. government views what *we* usually refer to as the 50 States. If you haven't yet read that Appendix entry, now would be a good time.

The U.S. Constitution allows our U.S. President, with the approval of our U.S. Senate, to compose and implement '*treaties*' with other countries. It then goes on to identify that the U.S. Constitution and the '*laws*' of the United States, along with these '*treaties*', become the law of the land and that our judges are to adjudicate accordingly.

What this means is that we are expected to live according to *not just* our U.S. Constitution and the '*laws*' written that are *supposed to be* in sync with the U.S. Constitution, but also to any '*treaties*' that are signed. Do you now understand how crucial it is that '*treaties*' such as NAFTA and CAFTA must be reviewed and critiqued by us and if unacceptable items are found then we must respond loudly and reject them soundly? Do you also understand that future '*treaties*' such as the one that would form the '*North American Union*' to '*compete*' with the recently formed '*European Union*' could result with the USofA becoming subservient to a government that is even '*larger*' and '*more powerful*' than even the current U.S. government? Could '*freedom*' possibly survive under an even more omnipotent government?

O. Watch-Dogging Government

Every law that our government writes should be scrutinized by *us* prior to it becoming law and then again if and when it *becomes* law.

There have been U.S. Congressmen who have proposed legislation that would require that any legislation written in Washington D.C. include the excerpt from the U.S. Constitution that empowers Congress to do what is contained in the legislation. That proposed legislation has still not passed. It's a terrific idea. Any ideas of why it hasn't yet passed?

There has been much talk about empowering the U.S. President with the '*Line Item Veto*' so that he could dig through legislation that has been put on his desk for his final signature so that he could cross out those items in that legislation which he deems '*unnecessary*' or '*pork barrel spending*', you know, all that '*extra*' spending that gets stuck in the legislation in order to '*buy*' the votes of specific legislators to '*sign on*' to the legislation. Another good idea? Many State Governors have that same '*Line Item Veto*' ability for use against legislation written by State legislators.

How about more laws that '*sunset*' or in other words automatically become invalid after a certain amount of time has passed?

How about some laws with regards to candidates, elected politicians, and government bureaucrats who '*lie*', '*cheat*', '*steal*' or '*infringe*'?

How about someone getting paid *bonus* for digging through existing laws and passing legislation to *invalidate* the old laws? Or how about *requiring* that a certain number of *old* laws be reviewed and eliminated before any *new* laws can be written?

Okay, I confess, I'm getting slap-happy …

P. Replace The Boundary Definitions Into Your State's Constitution

(If you don't know what I'm talking about then I know that you still haven't yet read Appendix 3…) I'd love to hear the excuses that liberals come up with for why we should not replace those boundary definitions. I cannot even begin to imagine what they might be. And while we're at it, how about replacing the '*Militia*' sections, too?

Q. Watch/Listen For Other '*Current*' Issues

There are sources out there where you can read or hear about current issues that need to be addressed. There may be one that catches your interest. A couple of recent issues include:
- Energy independence
- Bestowing those Rights that are guaranteed to U.S. citizens to illegals or foreigners (including non-American terrorists)
- There is so much estrogen not cleaned up from our city water supplies that the hormone levels of our adult males is being compromised. (Need I say more?)

R. Pick One of the Two Following Assignments and Get Back With Me With Your Results:

1. Consider the following:
   a. Given the following two quotes from our '*rulebook*':

"I do solemnly swear (or affirm) that I will support and defend the Constitution of the United States against all enemies, foreign and domestic; ..."

"Article. III. Section. 3. Treason against the United States, shall consist only in levying War against them, or in adhering to their Enemies, giving them Aid and Comfort."

b. And given the list from Chapter 2 of this book:

"Top Eleven Methods for Twisting the Meaning of Our Rulebook"

c. Exactly when does a person's behavior fall into the category of '*domestic enemy*' and thus be considered '*treason*'?

2. Explain how we can achieve a '*civilized society*' while still maintaining people's individual '*freedom*' without adopting as a way of life the '*moral foursome*' of '*not lying, not cheating, not stealing* and *not infringing*'?

And in the final analysis...

What will happen if we keep on down the road we are currently traveling and we don't turn this ship around? Perhaps the best answer that I can supply is to suggest some recommended reading. To answer that specific question I believe that Ayn Rand has provided the most accurate and complete answer.

Ayn Rand was a prolific writer during the twentieth century. Like my grandfather she too immigrated from Russia and all that its oppressive form of government entailed.

Her first novel *We The Living*, first published in 1936, was described by Rand:

"...as near to an autobiography as I will ever write."

The story revolves around the struggles of a thinking person who watches as her home country is taken over and devoured by people who believe as follows: '*the group must do whatever it takes*', that '*all in the group must enjoy equal results (and equal misery)*', and '*the group will make sure that all in the group see things the group's way*'. Another way to describe the story is '*living with communism*'.

Rand's most accomplished novel *Atlas Shrugged*, first published in 1957, was declared:

"...the most influential book of all time (after the Bible) in America, according to a joint survey by the Library of Congress and the Book-of-the-Month Club"[20]

The story is set in the USofA and shows in grand melodramatic style how government intervention along with the thought patterns of all those individuals who *support* that intervention will not only destroy the ability of any business to successfully produce products but will also force the creative individuals within our society to stop being creatively productive (because they finally refuse to be beaten down and exploited by all of the '*takers*' of this world). Ultimately, any progress that our society could make will end and our society will be sent plummeting in a downward spiral back towards the Stone Age.

Rand also wrote much non-fiction where she defined and described an entire philosophy that she called '*Objectivism*'. It is a deep and penetrating philosophy that seems to fit perfectly with the form of government that our Founding Fathers defined via the U.S. Constitution. Although I cannot say that I understand all of her '*Objectivism*', nor does she convince me to believe in all aspects that I think I do understand, the two novels that I have identified are magnificent in their ability to wave a warning flag to all of us who appreciate *freedom* and who recognize all of the benefits that *freedom* has to offer.

So is there a political issue that strikes your fancy?

And will you get up off of the couch?

Chapter 8

I Have The Right …

I've quoted earlier our Founding Fathers and the fact that they declared that we are born with "*unalienable Rights*". That phrase came straight from *The Declaration of Independence*. A word count of that document has the word "*right*" or "*rights*" appearing ten times. Although a few times when this word is used it functions as in the phrase "*it's the right thing to do*", most times it refers to different '*Rights*' that we as people have and finally that "*to secure these Rights, Governments are instituted*".

I've also quoted our U.S. Constitution a few different places where the word "*right*" or "*rights*" is used. A word count of *that* document has the word appearing fifteen times and each time it is done when enumerating specific '*Rights*' that we as people have *except* in the Ninth Amendment. There it states that just because *some* '*Rights*' are specifically listed in the U.S. Constitution it doesn't mean that the people don't have *other* Rights, too.

But what are these '*Rights*'? In fact, what is a '*Right*'?

My *Merriam-Webster Dictionary* has as one of its definitions for "*right*": "*something to which one has a just or lawful claim*".

My *Black's Law Dictionary* has as one of its definitions for "*right*": "*a power, privilege, faculty, or demand, inherent in one person and incident on another*". A second excerpt states: "*a capacity residing in one man of controlling, with the assent and the assistance of the state, the actions of others*".

I apologize that each of these definitions are rather vague to a normal person, kind of written in '*legalize*', but the ones I've listed are the clearest definitions offered.

And actually the definition listed in my *Black's Law Dictionary* goes on and on for nearly two full pages with another two pages listing specific "*Rights*" and their definitions such as the "*Right of privacy*" or the "*Right of survivorship*". These lengthy, intense, confusing and monotonous definitions are one more reason that we have '*friction*' between '*liberals*' and '*conservatives*'. The deeper I study the more I'm convinced that this single word is at the basis for much of our political debate.

I've stated earlier in this book that "*my Rights end where your nose begins*". I've built much of my book around the foursome of '*Rights*' that need to be protected, namely *"Life, Liberty, Property* and *Pursuit of Happiness"*. But have we really become specific enough that we are all in agreement regarding what is a *'Right'*? And no, we haven't.

In the upcoming Epilogue I'll be addressing the phrase *'moral obligation'* without dwelling much on its meaning (but instead just suggesting it as a *'brain teaser'*). A deep analysis of *that* phrase alongside a deep analysis of *'Rights'* are probably necessary for identifying what it really means to be a *'civilized society'*. However, those deep analyses are way beyond the scope of this book. What we *do* need to get our brains around is how different people view *'Rights'* in the most basic of terms. And I believe we've been given enough *'clues'* in the quotes that I've already listed.

Let's conduct a discussion around a specific issue that has been largely discussed over the past decade in our current society, as an example, in order to make our discussion understandable.

"I have the Right to Healthcare". Wow, now *that's* a mouthful.

By *my* way of thinking, in current American society, this statement is a *'shortcut'* or *'sound bite'* that purposely misleads people in order to *'change'* our society. Those of us who just want to be *'left alone'* (and who understand *'free-market capitalism'*) will shy away from anything having to do with the concept of *'government supplied Healthcare'* while those who want *'something for nothing'* will be up front and center fighting *for* it.

By *my* way of thinking people have the *Right* to pursue *good* health just as they have the *Right* to pursue *bad* health; people have the *Right* to pursue the purchase of healthcare and they have the *Right* to pursue the purchase of insurance to cover their healthcare expenses; and lastly, according to laws already passed, people cannot be refused *emergency* healthcare in the Emergency Rooms of America. Because of those Emergency Room laws government has declared *emergency* healthcare to be what some might refer to as a *'Right'*.

In the three preceding paragraphs I listed six *'Rights'*. Some of them fall neatly into the *'my Rights end where your nose begins'* category; others fall into that same category as long as you add *'money'* (or *'purchasing power'*) to the equation; one does *not* fit neatly because the government has *declared it* and it can only be accommodated if some folks *'give'* their expertise, their products, their services, to the Emergency Room patient, in the hopes that maybe somehow someday they can recoup the expenses and maybe even get paid for their knowledge and their labor; and the last one I referred to as a *'sound bite'*. The Emergency Room *'Right'* falls into what we might call the '*moral obligation*' category (see the upcoming Epilogue) while the '*sound bite*' falls into one or more of either the '*fuzzy liberal thinking*' category, the '*we still haven't learned our lesson that communism doesn't work*' category, the '*twist the meaning of our rulebook*' category or even more specifically the '*change the meaning of words*' category. Whichever of these four apply, it *also* falls into the '*something for nothing*' category. But using *my* thinking skills I am well aware that '*something for nothing*' only lives in fairy tale land; there are no free lunches; *somebody* ends up paying.

It's these '*somebody ends up paying*' *Rights* that are so troublesome for me. These '*government declares it*' *Rights* are the ones that fall outside the '*my Rights ... your nose ...*' category. These are the ones for which I wave the warning flag because these are the ones that invade my '*freedom*'.

Maybe it's the fact that the definitions in *Black's Law* include the phrases '*incident on another* [person]' and '*one man controlling, with the ... assistance of the state*' from where these '*somebody ends up paying*' *Rights* are justified. So maybe what we *really* need to do is to stop calling these things '*Rights*' and instead call them what they really are, namely '*government edicts*'.

Okay, so we may be changing the meaning of a word. Yes, *we* can play *that* game, too. But maybe in this case it would be a *good* thing. Maybe we'd really just be clarifying what has been until now a *fuzzy definition*. We may never persuade *Black's Law* to '*fix*' their own definition but at least if we could accentuate this difference in our own thoughts, our own discussions, then maybe we can regain some control over our government.

'*Rights*' versus '*government edicts*' ... '*My Rights end where your nose begins*'.

And regarding '*government supplied Healthcare*', what do I think? C'mon. Need I really spell it out?

'*Rights*' is a word that represents a mental concept and to accurately comprehend what a '*Right*' *is* requires good thinking skills. *My* understanding of what is a '*Right*' is something that I possess that no one else has the '*Right*' to take from me. But if somehow someone *does* justify taking it then an extremely extraordinary event must have taken place.

No one has the '*Right*' to take *my* '*Life*' because *my* '*Life*' belongs *to me*.

No one has the '*Right*' to take *my* '*Liberty*' because *my* '*Liberty*' *belongs to me*.

No one has the *'Right'* to take *my* *'Property'* because *my* *'Property'* *belongs to me.*

No one has the *'Right'* to deny me *my* *'Pursuit of Happiness'* ...

In other words, *my* *'Life'* is *my* *'Right'*, not yours. *My* *'Liberty'* is *my* *'Right'*, not yours. *My* *'Property'* is *mine*, not yours. *My* *'Pursuit of Happiness'* is *mine* ...

If someone takes my *'Life'* then an extremely extraordinary event has taken place, and we call that *"murder"*. If an enemy of our country takes my *'Life'* then an extremely extraordinary event has occurred and we call that *"war"*. But if my government takes my *'Life'* then *there darned well better have been an extremely extraordinary justification for having done so*, and we call that *'capital punishment'*.

In the first two situations in the paragraph above the result almost *'goes without saying'*, of course it is *"murder"* or *"war"*. But in the third situation, when the government does it, then we *must* qualify the result with *'there darned well better have been an extremely extraordinary justification for having done so'*.

And the same goes for my *'Liberty'*, my *'Property'*, and my *'Pursuit of Happiness'*; *there darned well better have been an extremely extraordinary justification...*

And I don't believe that under any stretch of the imagination that somebody wanting *'something for nothing'* fits into the *'there darned well better have been an extremely extraordinary justification...'* category.

Another idiom that is often heard when discussing *'Rights'* is to point out that *'what government can give, government can take away'*. Although we've repeatedly discussed how all that government has to give has been taken from value producers, in *this* discussion we're talking about *'Rights'* (which is a little bit different than all of the money that government spends). If government is behind granting a *'Right'* (which is the way that most other countries function) then government can also un-grant that *'Right'*. Just like me, if I choose to give (or donate) some of my Property to someone else then I should also be able to choose to no longer give (or donate) my Property. A giver always has the *'Right'* to stop giving.

So when the government is where *'Rights'* come from then the government is the giver thus the government can choose to no longer give. But remember in this country we have *'Rights'* because we were born, *not* because the government gave them to us. So again, are there specific *'Rights'* that aren't really *'Rights'* simply because someone in the government declares them so, or are they in fact *'government edicts'* (that '*somebody ends up paying*' for)?

'*Rights*' versus '*government edicts*' … '*My Rights end where your nose begins*'.

"*I have the Right to Healthcare*" is just another one of those issues that liberals have decided is their next best way to purchase votes from the '*woe is me*' crowd, the next best way to grab additional power from the capitalists, the next best way to obtain more control over '*the masses*', the next best way to guilt the '*haves*' into handing over more of their '*Property*'. The scenario is so darned predictable. Each election cycle the liberals must come up with a new '*crisis*', to divide us, to conquer us, to justify their own existence. Their buddies in the '*old*' media are always there to help push the agenda, to tell tales of those suffering hardship, to push the panic button so that the liberals will get listened to. But as I said it's the same ole' story. If liberals didn't perform these acts then no one would take them seriously; no one would listen to their latest rants.

"*I have the Right to Just Be Left Alone*" is my latest rant. Do you hear me liberals? Leave me alone!

There was a saying that I've heard repeatedly over the years, that "*if you're 18 and you* aren't *a liberal then something's wrong with you; and if you're 40 and you* are *a liberal then something's wrong with you.*" My new belief is that at any age if you're a liberal then …

And by the way, my *Merriam-Webster Dictionary* also has as one of its definitions for "*right*": "*political conservatives*". Indeed it is very common in today's society to refer to '*liberals*' as being on the '*left*' and '*conservatives*' as being on the '*right*'.

Thus we now have three basic descriptions for that same one word as exemplified by the phrases '*doing what is right*', '*people have unalienable Rights*', and '*conservatives are on the right*'. Could a study from where the word was originally derived show some significant connection between these three different descriptions? I'm not implying anything; just wondering.

Epilogue

When you '*talk*' about things with others you often don't really end up completing '*full thoughts*'. Hand gestures, facial expressions, interruptions by the other person and the other person '*finishing your sentence*' for you all contribute to the '*full thoughts*' not being completed. However, when you write something down you are forced, per the definition of a sentence, to state complete thoughts.

Then once written down and reread it can become more obvious when there are gaps in your paragraph building or when there is fuzziness or flaws in your thinking.

The writing of this book has helped me prove to myself that my thinking is sound. But even so I have found it necessary to reread it numerous times as a refresher course for myself and especially to keep myself '*sane*' when I am verbally pummeled with the fuzzy thinking of some that I encounter in our society.

I have also found that it has helped me to converse more '*kindly*' with those who oppose my views. My own deep understanding and my knowing that my thinking is complete helps me to choose my words more carefully and to make compelling arguments when confronted with opportunities to '*help others understand*' or (to say it less kindly) to '*beat back the ignorance*'.

And do you remember how earlier I said that we must keep '*freedom*' at the '*tip of our tongues*' and in the '*frontal lobe of our brains*'? And how I said that we need an army of "*polite ... augmented with strength, smarts, backbone, conviction and a diplomatically clever tongue*" people? Well, rereading this book helps to reinforce these conditions for me.

The nephew that I've mentioned a couple of times is now sixteen.

I also mentioned my Grandpa and how there were *three* stories that he told that I will never forget. One was "Fool me once, shame on you. Fool me twice, shame on me." The second was "Dey fool da people". But the third one was a different type of story, one that wasn't in the form of a '*short ditty*' that could be repeated at a moment's notice but instead it's a '*feeling*' that haunts my soul.

Grandpa told of how his brother had been shot in the back by the Russian Army because they had caught him with seeds in his pocket. His brother had simply wanted to plant a little garden. The family was hungry.

If you know the history of what the Russians did to the Ukrainians (the Ukraine having been the first country to be taken over by the Russians in their quest to build a Soviet empire) then you know that millions of Ukes were starved to death. That history as it has been relayed to me is so incredibly shocking and disturbing that I personally find it *as bad if not worse* than the stories we hear about the Holocaust.

I sat with my nephew at a restaurant for dinner this week and we both sat speechless when I asked him to consider what his Great Grandfather had done nearly a century ago, having traveled alone to a land on the other side of the world, at age sixteen. I thought to myself about the pain he must have felt, regarding his brother, about leaving his parents, siblings, cousins, friends and the home he had always known, and with only a fourth grade education. And I thought how horrible the fear must have been to motivate him to have made that journey.

He had only been sixteen, and now his Great Grandson is sixteen.

How bad can it get when a government demands complete compliance with their '*rules*'?

Survival is one of our most basic desires.

Every individual has a most basic desire to survive.

But so does our government. It wants to survive.

Then there's freedom, and the way it permeates the soul of each of us human beings, wanting desperately also for freedom to survive.

And for freedom's sake, the best guarantee that we've got, namely '*free market capitalism*', must also survive.

Is there a way for all these separate entities to all coexist and all survive? I believe that our Founding Fathers provided the tools if only we will get out there and use them.

Every time *you* allow the government additional power, or even to retain their current level of power, *you* are deciding that everyone else must be stripped of *more* of their freedoms. Are you ready to defend yourself and any beliefs that you might have that justify large or even larger government?

Remember that when a problem presents itself, in order to find a *real* solution that *really works* it makes sense to call on the '*experts*'. For the life of me I cannot understand why *anyone* would think that just because a person wins an election that he is '*expert*' at anything other than winning that particular election. Why would anyone think that this '*election winner*' is suddenly equipped with all of the knowledge and know how for solving all of the problems of each one of his constituents?

Perhaps now you can also see why conservatives have become completely disgusted with and mistrusting of the mainstream media. Historically journalists have been viewed as and referred to as the "*fourth branch of government*". It has been an accepted fact that the survivability of our society depends on an abundance of people out there digging up the facts (for us), assembling them (for us) and using logical thinking skills to portray (for us) what is really going on in our government.

What conservatives have discovered is that over the past several decades (at least) the mainstream media has been failing so completely at performing that job that a '*new*' media has evolved to fill the void. The '*old*' media has been horribly deficient in digging up facts about those in the government who are on '*their*' side while only digging up '*facts*' about their '*opponents*'. They have been horribly deficient in assembling and portraying what is occurring on '*their*' side as well as inserting their own *opinions* and claiming them to be '*facts*' when it comes to badmouthing their '*opponents*'.

Over the past several decades it has been repeatedly shown that high level media persons have used forged documents and represented them as authentic in their efforts to badmouth conservatives. They have been caught making up stories in their own efforts at notoriety. They have admitted to using (for accumulating their '*facts*') sources who have no credibility and whose '*facts*' could not be verified with a second source. They've led the charge repeatedly that '*the seriousness of the charge*' is sufficient ammunition for taking down a conservative implying that spurious allegations were enough to deem a particular conservative '*guilty enough*' to eliminate him from our midst (when their real goal has been to destroy each and every conservative simply because they are conservative). And all the while they seem determined to never write a negative phrase about anyone on '*their*' side but when something negative *is* uncovered then they dismiss it as '*no big deal*'.

As a result I urge you to take great care when you hear stories from the media. Recognize that all journalists do *not* have integrity and that some are pushing an agenda as opposed to digging up '*facts*' and verifying them as '*real facts*'. Because if we are to use what '*they*' present as facts in our most basic process of '*thinking*' and they turn out to *not* be facts or *not all of* the facts then you can see that our '*thinking*' will be corrupted and sabotaged right along with our '*civilized society*'.

Another sidebar that deserves mention, a phrase you might hear the deeper you plunge into this world of politics and political discussion. Because we as a country are '*moral*' many folks believe that we need to *endlessly prove it*, and perhaps because we as a country are the biggest and best then we have a '*moral obligation*' to help those less able to help themselves. This specific debate in our country dates back to our Founding Fathers and no doubt prior to that, so to think that this topic is one with an easy answer …

My opinion on this matter is that it is *truly commendable* to help others. However, the '*callus heartless ogre*' that apparently I am I still must question whether stealing money from my fellow citizens (an '*immoral*' act) in order to finance the said '*moral obligation*' is justified by the '*moral obligation*' or if it actually *negates* the morality of it. (Do you see much fun this '*thinking*' stuff can be?)

May I one last time state that stealing is hideously wrong. And even more so, *those people who think that stealing is acceptable if you can find someone more powerful to do the dirty work for you*, such as the government and their paid agents, or a democracy by "*voting*" for the thievery, or a street gang or street thug who has a gun pointed in your direction, *anyone who thinks that type of stealing is acceptable is*, in my view, *diabolically despicable.*

And that includes *stealing* my *Life* or my ability to sustain my life, or *stealing* my *Liberty* or freedom, or *stealing* my *Property* which includes an excessive slice of my paycheck, or *stealing* my *Pursuit of Happiness* which includes my not needing to surround myself with lawyers nor to have to pay a *sin tax* …

Also, there are many manipulators out there and those manipulators have many techniques for getting their way. One common method is one that I've heard described in several different ways, each using different words. But the way that I always remember it is by utilizing one particular *uncommon* yet kind of cool word along with two other words that are modified versions of that first word. Those three words along with definitions I found in my *Webster's Dictionary* are as follows. Note also the order in which the words are listed.

Thesis – "in logic, an unproved statement assumed as a premise"
Antithesis – "in rhetoric, an opposition or contrast of thoughts; … the exact opposite"
Synthesis – "in philosophy, deductive reasoning … from cause to effect, from a principle to its application"

Indeed, again, cryptic and confusing. So let me explain how it works.

A manipulator has a goal in mind that will somehow benefit him self, but how can he get his way? He manipulates by *declaring the existence of a problem* (usually describing it as a *crisis*). Then he *proposes a solution* (which is supposed to remedy the crisis). Then eventually the *solution is implemented* (which actually results in achieving the goal that the manipulator sought in the first place *regardless of whether* it really solves the problem that was declared in the "*thesis*").

With the above explanation in mind, consider how the media could be very instrumental in supporting the manipulations. The media could easily take an *issue* and turn it into a *crisis that must be addressed!* Then they could wave the banner of *a miracle in our midst* should we simply convince our government to implement some new law. Finally, they could then declare the crisis *resolved* once the new law is passed because they, the media, never again report on the issue; out of sight, out of mind, and thus most folks forget about it all. But often, because the declared problem *is not really resolved* by the new law, the media can then start waving the crisis banner again, claiming that *no one had really taken the issue seriously*, that *not enough money was spent*, that *no one really did enough to really resolve the crisis*. And the whole cycle begins again and it all digs us all deeper into those "*solutions*" that really only benefit the manipulator.

"*Fool me once, shame on you. Fool me twice, shame on me*". Don't get fooled. The manipulators and the media repeat this "*thesis - antithesis - synthesis*" scenario far more often than most of us might ever suspect. In fact, this is one of the most common methods used for political campaigns at election time; a candidate declares a *crisis that must be addressed*, then he proposes that if you'll elect him then *he'll work to resolve the crisis*. But you know, what's *really going on* here may be nothing more than *a manipulator who is trying to win an election and not a concerned citizen who is really trying to resolve the crisis that he claims to be concerned about*. So once again you can see the importance of *engaging your brain* instead of just reacting or of exploring your emotions.

Remember, regardless of what you discover is going on out there, *keep a level head.*

Finally, what will happen if we keep on down the road we are currently traveling and we don't turn this ship around? Any last gasp of *freedom* will be permanently, once and for all, wiped from our planet. And since we *all* know that the victors write (or rewrite) history, and since we *now* know that freedom's death will be *because* the *liars*, *cheats*, *thieves* and *infringers* have won, then we *also can be sure* that future history books will *tell lies* about what had once been known as the USofA.

The *immoral* victors will write that the USofA was a ridiculous experiment, that '*those people back then*' had the audacity to believe that individualism was something somehow sacred; that individual '*citizens*' were so self-centered, egotistical, narcissistic, and perverse that they thought that they could *choose* their own spouse, or whether they would have a spouse at all; that they could *decide for themselves* how many children they would sire; that they themselves could *select* where they would live, or where they would work, or even which career path they might follow. They'd refer to those '*dark days*' when '*freedom*' was attempted, back *before all 'citizens' accepted that the majority and the government knows best*, were nothing but a blip in human history...

APPENDIX

Our Rulebook

For your convenience I have taken the time and effort to include the following documents. I have painstakingly copied, word for word, uppercase letters versus lowercase letters, all the punctuation, etc. from my copy of these documents that was published in 1992 by the Commission of the Bicentennial of the United States Constitution, Washington, D.C. However, even though I might consider that these documents belong to all of us in the USofA, who knows what some liberal lawyer might dream up as a way to punish me for my opinions, sue me, or whatever. So I do not recommend using this appendix in any way other than for your convenience while reading this book.

CONSTITUTION OF THE UNITED STATES

We the People of the United States, in Order to form a more perfect Union, establish Justice, insure domestic Tranquility, provide for the common defence, promote the general Welfare, and secure the Blessings of Liberty to ourselves and our Posterity, do ordain and establish this Constitution for the United States of America.

Article. I.

Section. 1. All legislative Powers herein granted shall be vested in a Congress of the United States, which shall consist of a Senate and House of Representatives.

Section. 2. The House of Representatives shall be composed of Members chosen every second Year by the People of the several States, and the Electors in each State shall have Qualifications requisite for Electors of the most numerous Branch of the State Legislature.

No Person shall be a Representative who shall not have attained the

Age of twenty five Years, and been seven Years a Citizen of the United States, and who shall not, when elected, be an Inhabitant of that State in which he shall be chosen.

[Representatives and direct Taxes shall be apportioned among the several States which may be included within the Union, according to their respective Numbers, which shall be determined by adding to the whole Number of free Persons, including those bound to Service for a Term of Years, and excluding Indians not taxed, three fifths of all other Persons.][21] The actual Enumeration shall be made within three Years after the first Meeting of Congress of the United States, and within every subsequent Term of ten Years, in such Manner as they shall by Law direct. The number of Representatives shall not exceed one for every thirty Thousand, but each State shall have at Least one Representative; and until such enumeration shall be made, the State of New Hampshire shall be entitled to chuse three, Massachusetts eight, Rhode-Island and Providence Plantations one, Connecticut five, New York six, New Jersey four, Pennsylvania eight, Delaware one, Maryland six, Virginia ten, North Carolina five, South Carolina five, Georgia three.

When vacancies happen in the Representation of any State, the Executive Authority thereof shall issue Writs of Election to fill such Vacancies.

The House of Representatives shall chuse their Speaker and other Officers; and shall have the sole Power of Impeachment.

Section. 3. The Senate of the United States shall be composed of two Senators from each State, [chosen by the Legislature thereof,][22] for six years; and each Senator shall have one Vote.

Immediately after they shall be assembled in Consequence of the first Election, they shall be divided as equally as may be into three Classes. The Seats of the Senators of the first Class shall be vacated at the Expiration of the second Year, of the second Class at the Expiration of the fourth Year, and of the third Class at the Expiration of the sixth Year, so that one third may be chosen every second Year; [and if Vacancies happen by Registration, or otherwise, during the Recess of the Legislature of any State, the Executive thereof may make temporary Appointments until the next Meeting of the Legislature, which shall then fill such Vacancies.][23]

No person shall be a Senator who shall not have attained the Age of thirty Years, and been nine Years a Citizen of the United States, and who shall not, when elected, be an Inhabitant of the State for shich he shall be chosen.

The Vice President of the United States shall be President of the

Senate, but shall have no Vote, unless they be equally divided.

The Senate shall chuse their Officers, and also a President pro tempore, in the Absence of the Vice President, or when he shall exercise the Office of President of the United States.

The Senate shall have sole Power to try all Impeachments. When sitting for that Purpose, they shall be on Oath or Affirmation. When the President of the United States is tried, the Chief Justice shall preside: And no Person shall be convicted without the Concurrence of two thirds of the Members present.

Judgment in the Cases of Impeachment shall not extend further than to removal from Office, and disqualification to hold and enjoy ad Office of honor, Trust or Profit under the United States; but the Party convicted shall nevertheless be liable and subject to Indictment, Trial, Judgment and Punishment, according to Law.

Section. 4. The Times, Places and Manner of holding Elections for Senators and Representatives, shall be prescribed in each State by the Legislature thereof; but the Congress may at any time by law make or alter such Regulations, except as to the Places of chusing Senators.

The Congress shall assemble at least once in every Year, and such Meeting shall be [on the first Monday in December,][24] unless they shall by Law appoint a different Day.

Section. 5. Each House shall be the Judge of the Elections, Returns and Qualifications of its own Members, and a Majority of each shall constitute a Quorum to do Business; but a smaller Number may adjourn from day to day, and may be authorized to compel the Attendance of absent Members, in such Manner, and under such Penalties as each House may provide.

Each House may determine the Rules of its Proceedings, punish its Members for disorderly Behaviour, and, with the Concurrence of two thirds, expel a Member.

Each House shall keep a Journal of its Proceedings, and from time to time publish the same, excepting such Parts as may in their Judgment require Secrecy; and the Yeas and Nays of the Members of either House on any question shall, at the Desire of one fifth of those Present, be entered on the Journal.

Neither House, during the Session of Congress, shall, without the Consent of the other, adjourn for more than three days, nor to any other Place than that in which the two Houses shall be sitting.

Section. 6. The Senators and Representatives shall receive a Compensation for their Services, to be ascertained by Law, and paid out of the Treasury of the United States. They shall in all Cases, except Treason, Felony and Breach of the Peace, be privileged from Arrest during their Attendance at the Session of their respective Houses, and in going to and returning from the same; and for any Speech or Debate in either House, they shall not be questioned in any other Place.

No Senator or Representative shall, during the Time for which he was elected, be appointed to any civil Office under the Authority of the United States, which shall have been created, or the Emoluments whereof shall have been encreased during such time; and no Person holding any Office under the United States, shall be a Member of either House during his Continuance of Office.

Section. 7. All Bills for raising Revenue shall originate in the House of Representatives; but the Senate may propose or concur with Amendments as on other Bills.

Every Bill which shall have passed the House of Representatives and the Senate, shall, before it becomes Law, be presented to the President of the United States; If he approve he shall sign it, but if not he shall return it, with his Objections to that House in which it shall have originated, who shall enter the Objections at large on their Journal, and proceed to reconsider it. If after such Reconsideration two thirds of that House shall agree to pass the Bill, it shall be sent, together with the objections, to the other House, by which it shall likewise be reconsidered, and if approved by two thirds of that House, it shall become Law. But in all such Cases the Votes of both Houses shall be determined by Yeas and Nays, and the Names of the Persons voting for and against the Bill shall be entered on the Journal of each House respectively. If any Bill shall not be returned by the President within ten Days (Sundays excepted) after it shall have been presented to him, the Same shall be a Law, in like Manner as if he had signed it, unless the Congress by their Adjournment prevent its Return, in which Case it shall not be Law.

Every Order, Resolution, or Vote to which the Concurrence of the Senate and House of representatives may be necessary (except on a question of Adjournment) shall be presented to the President of the United States; and before the Same shall take Effect, shall be approved by him, or being disapproved by him, shall be repassed by two thirds of the Senate and House of Representatives, according to the Rules and Limitations prescribed in the Case of a Bill.

Section. 8. The Congress shall have Power To lay and collect Taxes, Duties, Imposts and Excises, to pay the Debts and provide for the common Defense and general Welfare of the United States; but all Duties, Imposts and Excises shall be uniform throughout the United States;

To borrow Money on the credit of the United States;

To regulate Commerce with foreign Nations, and among the several States, and with the Indian Tribes;

To establish an uniform Rule of naturalization, and uniform Laws on the subject of Bankruptcies throughout the United States;

To coin Money, regulate the Value thereof, and of foreign Coin, and fix the Standard of Weights and Measures;

To provide for the Punishment of counterfeiting the Securities and current Coin of the United States;

To establish Post Offices and post Roads;

To promote the Progress of Science and useful Arts, by securing for limited Times to Authors and Inventors the exclusive Right to their respective Writings and Discoveries;

To constitute Tribunals inferior to the supreme Court;

To define and punish Piracies and Felonies committed on the high Seas, and Offenses against the Law of Nations;

To declare War, grant Letters of Marque and Reprisal, and make Rules concerning Captures on Land and Water;

To raise and support Armies, but no Appropriation of Money to Use shall be for a longer Term than two Years;

To provide and maintain a Navy;

To provide for calling forth the Militia to execute the Laws of the Union, suppress Insurrections and repel Invasions;

To provide for organizing, arming, and disciplining, the Militia, and for governing such part of them as may be employed in the Service of the United States, reserving to the States respectively, the Appointment of the Officers, and the Authority of training the Militia according to the discipline prescribed by Congress;

To exercise exclusive Legislation in all Cases whatsoever, over such District (not exceeding ten miles square) as may, by Cession of particular States, and the Acceptance of Congress, become the Seat of the Government of the United States, and to exercise like Authority over all Places purchased by the Consent of the Legislature of the State in which the Same shall be, for the Erection of Forts, Magazines, Arsenals, dock-Yards and other needful Buildings; - And

To make all Laws which shall be necessary and proper for carrying into execution the foregoing Powers, and all other Powers vested by this

Constitution in the Government of the United States, or in Department or Officer thereof.

Section. 9. The Migration or Importation of such Persons as any of the States now existing shall think proper to admit, shall not be prohibited by Congress prior to the Year one thousand eight hundred and eight, but a Tax or duty may be imposed on such Importation, not exceeding ten dollars for each person.

The Privilege of the Writ of Habeas Corpus shall not be suspended, unless when in Cases of Rebellion or Invasion the public Safety may require it.

No Bill of Attainder or ex post facto Law shall be passed.

No Capitation, or other direct, Tax shall be laid, unless in Proportion to the Census or Enumeration herein before directed to be taken.[25]

No Tax or Duty shall be laid on Articles exported from any State.

No Preference shall be given by any Regulation of Commerce or Revenue to the Ports of one State over those of another: nor shall Vessels boud to, or from, one State, be obliged to enter, clear, or pay Duties in another.

No Money shall be drawn from the Treasury, but in Consequence of Appropriations made by Law; and a regular Statement and Account of the Receipts and Expenditures of all public Money shall be published form time to time.

No Title of Nobility shall be granted by the United States: And no Person holding any Office of Profit or Trust under them, shall, without the Consent of Congress, accept any present, Emolument, Office, or Title, of any kind whatever, from any King, Prince, or Foreign State.

Section. 10. No State shall enter into any Treaty Alliance, or Confederation; grant Letters of Marque and Reprisal; coin Money; emit Bills of Credit; make any Thing but gold and silver Coin a Tender in payment of Debts; pass any Bill of Attainder, ex post facto Law, or Law impairing the obligation of Contracts, or grant any Title of Nobility.

No State shall, without the Consent of the Congress, lay any Imposts or Duties on Imports or Exports, except what may be absolutely necessary for executing it's inspection Laws: and the net Produce of all Duties and Imposts, laid by any State on Imports and Exports, shall be for the Use of the Treasury of the United States; and all such Laws shall be subject to the Revision and Controul of the Congress.

No State shall, without the Consent of Congress, lay any Duty of Tonnage, keep Troops, or Ships of War in time of Peace, enter into any

Agreement of Compact with another State, or with a foreign Power, or engage in War, unless actually invaded, or in such imminent Danger as will not admit of delay.

Article. II.

Section. 1. The executive Power shall be vested in a President of the United States of America. He shall hold the Office during the Term of four Years, and, together with the Vice President, chosen for the same Term, be elected, as follows

Each State shall appoint, in such Manner as Legislature thereof may direct, a Number of Electors, equal to the whole Number of Senators and Representatives to which the State may be entitled in the Congress: but no Senator or Representative, or Person holding an Office of Trust or Profit under the United States, shall be appointed an Elector.

[The Electors shall meet in their respective States, and vote by Ballot for two Persons, of whom one at lease shall not be an Inhabitant of the same State with themselves. And they shall make a List of all the Persons voted for, and of the Number of Votes for each; which List they shall sign and certify, and transmit sealed to the Seat of the Government of the United States, directed to the President of the Senate. The President of the Senate shall, in the Presence of the Senate and House of Representatives, open all the Certificates, and the Votes shall then be counted. The Person having the greatest Number of Votes shall be President, if such Number be a Majority of the whole Number of Electors appointed; and if there be more than one who have such a Majority, and have an equal Number of Votes, then the House of Representatives shall immediately chuse by Ballot one of them for President; and if no Person have a Majority, then from the five highest on the List the House shall in like Manner chuse the President. But in chusing the President, the Votes shall be taken by States, the Representation from each State having one Vote; A quorum for this Purpose shall consist of a Member or Members from two thirds of the States, and a Majority of all the States shall be necessary to a Choice. In every Case, after the Choice of the President, the Person having the greatest Number of Votes of the Electors shall be the Vice President. But if there should remain two or more who have equal Votes, the Senate shall chuse from them by Ballot the Vice President.][26]

The Congress may determine the Time of chusing the Electors, and the Day on which they shall give their Votes; which Day shall be the same throughout the Unites States.

No Person except a natural born Citizen, or a Citizen of the United States, at the time of the Adoption of this Constitution, shall be eligible to the Office of the President; neither shall any person be eligible to that Office who shall not have attained to the Age of thirty five Years, and been fourteen Years a Resident within the United States.

[In Case of the Removal of the President from Office, or of his Death, Resignation, or Inability to discharge the Powers and Duties of the said Office, the Same shall devolve on the Vice President, and the Congress may by Law provide for the Case of Removal, Death, Resignation or Inability, both of the President and Vice President, declaring what Officer shall then act as President, and such Officer shall act accordingly, until Disability be removed, or a President shall be elected.][27]

The President shall, at stated Times, receive for his Services, a Compensation, which shall neither be increased nor diminished during the Period for which he shall have been elected, and he shall not receive within the Period any other Emolument from the United States, or any of them.

Before he enter on the Execution of his Office, he shall take the following Oath or Affirmation: - "I do solemnly swear (or affirm) that I will faithfully execute the Office of President of the United States, and will to the best of my Ability, preserve, protect and defend the Constitution of the United States."

Section. 2. The President shall be Commander in Chief of the Army and Navy of the United States, and of the Militia of the several States, when called into the actual Service of the United States; he may require the Opinion, in writing, of the principal Officer in each of the executive Departments, upon any Subject relating to the Duties of their respective Offices, and he shall have Power to grant Reprieves and Pardons for Offenses against the United States, except in Cases of Impeachment.

He shall have Power, by and with the Advice and Consent of the Senate, to make Treaties, provided two thirds of the Senators present concur; and he shall nominate, and by and with the Advice and Consent of the Senate, shall appoint Ambassadors, other public Ministers and Consuls, Judges of the supreme Court, and all other Officers of the United States, whose Appointments are not herein otherwise provided for, and which shall be established by Law: but the Congress may be Law vest the Appointment of such inferior Officers, as they think proper, in the President alone, in the Courts of Law, or in the Heads of Departments.

The President shall have Power to fill up all Vacancies that may happen curing the Recess of the Senate, by granting Commissions which shall expire at the End of their next Session.

Section. 3. He shall from time to time given to the Congress Information of the State of the Union, and recommend to their Consideration such Measures as he shall judge necessary and expedient; he may, on extraordinary Occasions, convene both Houses, or either of them, with Respect to the Time of Adjournment, he hay adjourn them to such Time as he shall think proper; he shall receive Ambassadors and other public Ministers; he shall take Care that the Laws be faithfully executed, and shall Commission all the Officers of the United States.

Section. 4. The President, Vice President and all civil Officers of the United States, shall be removed from Office on Impeachment for, and Conviction of, Treason, Bribery, or other high Crimes and Misdemeanors.

Article. III.

Section. 1. The judicial Power of the United States, shall be vested in one supreme Court, and in such inferior Courts as the Congress may from time to time ordain and establish. The Judges, both of the supreme and inferior Courts, shall hold their Offices during good Behaviour, and shall, at stated Times, receive for their Services, a Compensation, which shall not be diminished during the Continuance in Office.

Section. 2. The judicial Power shall extend to all Cases, in Law and Equity, arising under this Constitution, the Laws of the United States, and their Treaties made, or which shall be made, under their Authority; - to all Cases affecting Ambassadors, other public Ministers and Consuls; - to all Cases of admiralty and maritime Jurisdiction; - to Controversies to which the United States shall be a party; - to Controversies between two or more States; - [between a State and Citizens of another State; -]28 between Citizens of different States, - between Citizens of the same State claiming lands under Grants of different States, [and between a State, or the Citizens thereof, and foreign States, Citizens or Subjects.]29

In all Cases affecting Ambassadors, other public Ministers and Consuls, and those in which a State shall be a Party, the supreme Court shall have original Jurisdiction. In all the other Cases before mentioned, the supreme Court shall have appellate Jurisdiction, both as to Law and Fact, with such Exceptions, and under such Regulations as the Congress shall make.

The Trial of all Crimes, except in Cases of Impeachment; shall be by Jury; and such Trial shall be held in the State where the said Crimes shall have been committed; but when mot committed within any State, the Trial shall be at such Place or Places as Congress may by Law have directed.

Section. 3. Treason against the United States, shall consist only in levying War against them, or in adhering to their Enemies, giving them Aid and Comfort. No Person shall be convicted of Treason unless on the Testimony of two Witnesses to the same overt Act, or on Confession in open Court.

The Congress shall have power to declare the Punishment of Treason, but no Attainder of Treason shall work Corruption of Blood, or Forfeiture except during the Life of the Person attained.

Article. IV.

Section. 1. Full Faith and Credit shall be given in each State to the public Acts, Records, and judicial Proceedings of every other State; And the Congress may by general Laws prescribe the Manner in which such Acts, Records and Proceedings shall be proved, and the Effect thereof.

Section. 2. The Citizens of each State shall be entitled to all Privileges and Immunities of Citizens in the several States.

A Person charged in any State with Treason, Felony, or other Crime, who shall flee from Justice, and be found in another State, shall on Demand of the executive Authority of the State from which he fled, be delivered up, to be removed to the State having Jurisdiction of the Crime.

[No Person held to the Service of Labour in one State, under the Laws thereof, escaping into another, shall, in Consequence of any Law or Regulation therein, be discharged from such Service or Labour, but shall be delivered up on Claim of the Party to whom such Service or Labour may be due.][30]

Section. 3. New States may be admitted by the Congress into the Union; but no new State shall be formed or erected within the Jurisdiction of any other State; nor any State be formed by the Junction of two or more States; nor any States, without the Consent of the Legislatures of the States concerned as well as of the Congress.

The Congress shall have Power to dispose of and make all needful Rules and Regulations respecting the Territory or other Property belonging to the United States; and nothing in the Constitution shall be construed as to Prejudice any Claims of the United States, or of any particular State.

Section. 4. The United States shall guarantee to every State in this Union a Republican Form of Government, and shall protect each of them against Invasion; and on Application of the Legislature, or of the Executive (when the Legislature cannot be convened) against domestic Violence.

Article. V.

The Congress, whenever two thirds of both Houses shall deem it necessary, shall propose Amendments to this Constitution, or, on the Application of the Legislatures of two thirds of the several States, shall call a Convention for proposing Amendments, which, in either Case, shall be valid to all Intents and Purposes, as part of this Constitution, when ratified by the Legislatures of three fourths of the several States, or by Conventions in three fourths thereof, as the one or the other Mode of Ratification may be proposed by the Congress; Provided that no Amendment which may be prior to the Year One thousand eight hundred and eight shall in any Manner affect the first and fourth Clauses in the Ninth Section of the first Article; and that no State, without its Consent, shall be deprived of it's equal Suffrage in the Senate.

Article. VI.

All debts contracted and Engagements entered into, before the Adoption of this Constitution, shall be as valid against the United States under this Constitution, as under the Confederation.

This Constitution, and the Laws of the United States which shall be made Pursuance thereof; and all Treaties made, or which shall be made, under the Authority of the United States, shall be the supreme Law of the Land; and the Judges in every State shall be bound thereby, any Thing in the Constitution or Laws of any State to the Contrary notwithstanding.

The Senators and Representatives before mentioned, and the Members of the several State Legislatures, and all executive and judicial Officers, both of the United States and the several States, shall be bound by Oath or Affirmation, to support this Constitution; but no religious Test shall ever be required as a Qualification to any Office or public Trust under the United States.

Article. VII.

The Ratification of the Conventions of nine States, shall be sufficient for the Establishment of this Constitution between the States so ratifying the Same.

Done in Convention by the Unanimous Consent of the States present the Seventeenth Day of September in the Year of the Lord on thousand seven hundred and Eighty seven and of the Independence of the United States of America the Twelfth In Witness whereof We have hereunto subscribed our Names,

G. Washington – Presid.
And deputy from : Virginia

New Hampshire	John Langdon
	Nicolas Gilman
Massachusetts	Nathaniel Gorham
	Rufus King
Connecticut	Wm. Saml. Johnson
	Roger Sherman
New York	Alexander Hamilton
New Jersey	Wil: Livingston
	David Brearley
	Wm. Paterson
	Jona: Dayton
Pennsylvania	B Franklin
	Thomas Mifflin
	Robt Morris
	Geo. Clymer
	Thos. FitzSimons
	Jared Ingersoll
	James Wilson
	Gouv Morris

Delaware	Geo. Read
	Gunning Bedford jun
	John Dickinson
	Richard Bassett
	Jaco: Broom
Maryland	James McHenry
	Dan of St Thos.
	Jenifer
	Danl Carroll
Virgina	John Blair-
	James Madison Jr.
North Carolina	Wm. Blount
	Richd. Dobbs Spaight
	Hu Williamson
South Carolina	J. Rutledge
	Charles Cotesworth
	Pinckney
	Pierce Butler
Georgia	William Few
	Abr Baldwin

Attest William Jackson Secretary

AMENDMENTS TO THE CONSTITUTION OF THE UNITED STATES OF AMERICA

Amendment I.[31]

Congress shall make no law respecting an establishment of religion, or prohibiting the free exercise thereof; or abridging the freedom of speech, or of the press, or the right of the people peaceably to assemble, and to petition the Government for a redress of grievances.

Amendment II.

A well regulated Militia, being necessary to the security of a free State, the right of the people to keep and bear Arms, shall not be infringed.

Amendment III.

No Soldier shall, in time of peace be quartered in any house, without the consent of the Owner, nor in time of war, but in a manner to be prescribed by law.

Amendment IV.

The right of the people to be secure in their persons, houses, papers, and effects, against unreasonable searches and seizures, shall not be violated, and no Warrants shall issue, but upon probable cause, supported by Oath or affirmation, and particularly describing the place to be searched, and the persons or things to be seized.

Amendment V.

No person shall be held to answer for a capital, or otherwise infamous crime, unless on a presentment or indictment of a Grand Jury, except in cases arising in the land or naval forces, or in the Militia, when in actual service in time of War or public danger, nor shall any person be subject for the same offence to be twice put in jeopardy of life or limb, not shall be compelled in any criminal case to be a witness against himself; nor be deprived of life, liberty, or property, without due process of law; nor shall private property be taken for public use without just compensation.

Amendment VI.

In all criminal prosecutions, the accused shall enjoy the right to a speedy and public trial, by an impartial jury of the State and district wherein the crime shall have been committed; which district shall be previously ascertained by law, and to be informed of the nature and cause of the accusation; to be confronted with the witnesses against him; to have compulsory process for obtaining witnesses in his favor, and to have the assistance of counsel for his defence.

Amendment VII.

In Suits at common law, where the value in controversy shall exceed twenty dollars, the right of trial by jury shall be preserved, and no fact tried by a jury shall be otherwise re-examined in any Court of the United States, than according to the rules of common law.

Amendment VIII.

Excessive bail shall not be required, nor excessive fines imposed, nor cruel and unusual punishments inflicted.

Amendment IX.

The enumeration in the Constitution of certain rights shall not be construed to deny or disparage others retained by the people.

Amendment X.

The powers not delegated to the United States by the Constitution, nor prohibited by it to the States, are reserved to the States respectively, or to the people.

Amendment XI.[32]

The Judicial power of the United States shall not b construed to extend to any suit in law or equity, commenced or prosecuted against one of the United States by Citizens of another State, or by Citizens or Subjects of any Foreign State.

Amendment XII.[33]

The Electors shall meet in their respective states, and vote by ballot for President and Vice President, one of whom, at least, shall not be an inhabitant of the same state with themselves; they shall name in their ballots the person voted for as President, and in distinct ballots the person voted for as Vice-President, and they shall make distinct lists of all persons voted for as President, and of all persons voted for as Vice-President, and of the number of votes for each, which lists they shall sign and certify, and transmit sealed to the seat of the government of the United States, directed to the President of the Senate; - The President of the Senate shall, in the presence of the Senate and House of Representatives, open all the certificates and the votes shall then be counted; - The person having the greatest number of votes for President, shall be the President, if such number be a majority of the whole number of Electors appointed; and if no person have such a majority, then from the persons having the highest numbers not exceeding three on the list of those voted for as President, the House of Representatives shall choose immediately, by ballot, the President. But in choosing the President, the votes shall be taken by states, the representation from each state having one vote; a quorum for this purpose shall consist of a member or members from two-thirds of the states, and a majority of all the states shall be necessary to a choice. [And if the House of Representatives shall not choose a President whenever the right of choice shall devolve upon them, before the fourth day of March next following, then the Vice-President shall act as President, as in the case of the death or other constitutional disability of the President -][34] The person having the greatest number of votes as Vice-President, shall be the Vice-President, if such number be a majority of the whole number of Electors appointed, and if no person have a majority, then from the two highest numbers on the list, the Senate shall choose the Vice-President; a quorum for the purpose shall consist of two-thirds of the whole number of Senators, and a majority of the whole number shall be necessary to a choice. But no person constitutionally ineligible to the office of President shall be eligible to that of Vice-President of the United States.

Amendment XIII.[35]

Section 1. Neither slavery nor involuntary servitude, except as a punishment for crime whereof the party shall have been duly convicted, shall exist within the United States, or any place subject to their jurisdiction.

Section 2. Congress shall have power to enforce this article by appropriate legislation.

Amendment XIV.[36]

Section 1. All persons born or naturalized in the United States and subject to the jurisdiction thereof, are citizens of the United States and of the State wherein they reside. No State shall make or enforce any law which shall abridge the privileges or immunities of citizens of the United States; nor shall any State deprive any person of life, liberty, or property, without due process of law; nor deny to any person within the jurisdiction the equal protection of the laws.

Section 2. Representatives shall be appointed among the several States according to their respective numbers, counting the whole number of persons in each State, excluding Indians not taxed. But when the right to vote at an election for the choice of electors for President and Vice President of the United States, Representatives in Congress, the Executive and Judicial officers of a State, or the members of the Legislature thereof, is denied to any of the male inhabitants of such State, being twenty-one years of age, and citizens of the United States, or in any way abridged, except for participation in rebellion, or other crime, the basis of representation therein shall be reduced in the proportion which the number of such male citizens shall bear to the whole number of male citizens twenty-one years of age in such State.

Section 3. No person shall be a Senator or Representative in Congress, or elector of President and Vice President, or hold any office, civil or military, under the United States, or under any State, who, having previously taken an oath, as a member of Congress, or as an officer of the United States, or as a member of any State legislature, or as an executive or judicial officer of any State, to support the Constitution of the United States, shall have engaged in insurrection of rebellion against the same, or given aid or comfort to the enemies thereof. But Congress may by a vote of two-thirds of each House, remove such disability.

Section 4. The validity of the public debt of the United States, authorized by law, including debts incurred for payment of pensions and bounties for services in suppressing insurrection or rebellion, shall not be questioned. But neither the United States nor any State shall assume or pay any debt or obligation incurred in aid of insurrection or rebellion against the United States, or any claim for the loss or emancipation of any slave; but all debts, obligations and claims shall be held illegal and void.

Section 5. The Congress shall have power to enforce, by appropriate legislation, the provisions of this article.

Amendment XV.[37]

Section 1. The right of the citizens of the United States to vote shall not be denied or abridged by the United States or by any State on account of race, color, or previous condition of servitude.

Section 2. The Congress shall have the power to enforce this article by appropriate legislation.

Amendment XVI.[38]

The Congress shall have the power to lay and collect taxes on incomes, from whatever source derived, without apportionment among the several States, and without regard to any census or enumeration.

Amendment XVII.[39]

The Senate of the United States shall be composed of two Senators from each State, elected by the people thereof, for six years; and each Senator shall have one vote. The electors in each State shall have the qualifications requisite for electors off the most numerous branch of the State legislatures.

When vacancies happen in the representation of any State in the Senate, the executive authority of such State shall issue writs of election to fill such vacancies: *Provided*, That the legislature of any State may empower the executive thereof to make temporary appointments until the people fill the vacancies by election as the legislature may direct.

This amendment shall not be so construed as to affect the election or term of any Senator chosen before it becomes valid as part of the Constitution.

Amendment XVIII.[40]

[**Section 1.** After one year from the ratification of this article the manufacture, sale, or transportation of intoxicating liquors within, the importation thereof into, or the exportation thereof from the United States and all territory subject to the jurisdiction thereof for beverage purposes is hereby prohibited.

Section 2. The Congress and the several States shall have the concurrent power to enforce this article by appropriate legislation.

Section 3. This article shall be inoperative unless it shall have been ratified as an amendment to the Constitution by the legislatures of the several States, as provided in the Constitution, within seven years from the date of the submission hereof to the States by the Congress.]

Amendment XIX.[41]

The right of citizens of the United States to vote shall not be denied or abridged by the United States or by any State on account of sex.

Congress shall have the power to enforce this article by appropriate legislation.

Amendment XX.[42]

Section 1. The terms of the President and Vice President shall end at noon on the 20th day of January, and the terms of Senators and Representatives at noon on the 3d day of January, of the years in which such terms would have ended if this article had not been ratified; and the terms of their successors shall then begin.

Section 2. The Congress shall assemble at least once in every year, and such meeting shall begin at noon on the 3d day of January, unless they shall by law appoint a different day.

Section 3. If, at the time fixed for the beginning of the term of President, the President elect shall have died, the Vice President elect shall become President. If a President shall not have been chosen before the time fixed for the beginning of his term, or if the President elect shall have failed to qualify, then the Vice President elect shall act as President until a President shall have qualified; and the Congress may by law provide for the case wherein neither a President elect nor a Vice President elect shall have qualified, declaring who shall then act as President, or the manner in which one who is to act shall be selected, and such person shall act accordingly until a President or Vice President shall have qualified.

Section 4. The Congress may by law provide for the case of the death of any of the persons from whom the House of Representatives may choose a President whenever the right of choice shall have devolved upon them, and for the case of death of any of the persons from whom the Senate may choose a Vice President whenever the right of choice shall have devolved upon them.

Section 5. Sections 1 and 2 shall take effect on the 15th day of October following the ratification of this article.

Section 6. This article shall be inoperative unless it shall have been ratified as an amendment to this Constitution by the legislatures of three-fourths of the several States within seven years from the date of its submission.

Amendment XXI.[43]

Section 1. The eighteenth article of amendment to this Constitution of the United States is hereby repealed.

Section 2. The transportation or importation into any State, Territory, or possession of the United States for delivery or use therein of intoxicating liquors, in violation of the laws, thereof, is hereby prohibited.

Section 3. This article shall be inoperative unless it shall have been ratified as an amendment to the Constitution by conventions in the several States, as provided in the Constitution, within seven years from the date of the submission hereof to the States by the Congress.

Amendment XXII.[44]

Section 1. No person shall be elected to the office of President more than twice, and no person who has held the office of President, or acted as President, for more than two years of a term to which some other person was elected President shall be elected to the office of President more than once. But this Article shall not apply to any person holding the office of President when this Article was proposed by Congress, and shall not prevent any person who may be holding the office of President, or acting as President, during the term in which this Article becomes operative from holding the office of President or acting as President during the remainder of such term.

Section 2. This article shall be inoperative unless it shall have been ratified as an amendment to this Constitution by the legislatures of three-fourths of the several States within seven years from the date of its submission to the States by the Congress.

Amendment XXIII.[45]

Section 1. The District constituting the seat of Government of the United States shall appoint in such manner as the Congress may direct:

A number of electors of President and Vice President equal to the whole number of Senators and Representatives in Congress to which the District would be entitled if it were a State, but in no event more than the least populace State; they shall be in addition to those appointed by the States, but they shall be considered, for the purposes of the election of the President and Vice President, to be electors appointed by a State; and they shall meet in the District and perform such duties as provided by the twelfth article of amendment.

Section 2. The Congress shall have power to enforce this article by appropriate legislation.

Amendment XXIV.[46]

Section 1. The right of the citizens of the United States to vote in any primary or other election for President or Vice President, for electors for President or Vice President, or for Senator or Representative in Congress, shall not be denied or abridged by the United States or any State by reason of failure to pay any poll tax or other tax.

Section 2. The Congress shall have power to enforce this article by appropriate legislation.

Amendment XXV.[47]

Section 1. in case of the removal of the President form office or his death or resignation, the Vice president shall become President.

Section 2. Whenever there is a vacancy in the office of the Vice President, the President shall nominate a Vice President who shall take office upon confirmation by a majority of both Houses of Congress.

Section 3. Whenever the President transmits to the President pro tempore of the Senate and the Speaker of the House of Representatives his written declaration that he is unable to discharge the powers and duties of his office, and until he transmits to them a written declaration to the contrary, such powers and duties shall be discharged by the Vice President as Acting President.

Section 4. Whenever the Vice President and a majority of either the principal officers of the executive departments or of such other bodies as Congress may by law provide, transmit to the President pro tempore of the Senate and the Speaker of the House of Representatives their written declaration that the president is unable to discharge the powers and duties of his office, the Vice president shall immediately assume the powers and duties of the office as Acting President.

Thereafter, when the President transmits to the President pro tempore of the Senate and the Speaker of the House of Representatives his written declaration that no inability exists, he shall resume the powers and duties of his office unless the Vice President and a majority of either the principal officers of the executive department or of such other body as Congress may by law provide, transmit within four days to the President pro tempore of the Senate and the Speaker of the House of Representatives their written declaration that the President is unable to discharge the powers and duties of his office. Thereupon Congress shall decide the issue, assembling within forty-eight hours for that purpose if not in session. If the Congress, within twenty-one days after receipt of the latter written declaration, or, if Congress is not in session, within twenty-one days after Congress is required to assemble, determines by two-thirds vote of both Houses that the President is unable to discharge the powers and duties of his office, the Vice President shall continue to discharge the same as Acting President; otherwise, the President shall resume the powers and duties of his office.

Amendment XXVI.[48]

Section 1. The right of citizens of the United States, who are eighteen years of age or older, to vote shall not be denied or abridged by the United States or by and State on account of age.

Section 2. The Congress shall have power to enforce this article by appropriate legislation.

Amendment XXVII.[49]

No law, varying the compensation for the services of the Senators and Representatives, shall take effect, until an election of Representatives shall have intervened.

Excerpts from:

THE COMMUNIST MANIFESTO
Karl Marx
And
Friedrich Engels

The above named book, after 100 years, was translated into English by Paul M. Sweezy and published by the Monthly Review Press of New York. Below is a direct excerpt from that translation, and is more commonly known as the "*Ten Planks of Communism*":

"

1. Abolition of property in land and application of all rents of land to public purposes.
2. A heavy progressive or graduated income tax.
3. Abolition of all right of inheritance.
4. Confiscation of property of emigrants and rebels.
5. Centralization of credit in the hands of the State, by means of a national band with State capital and an exclusive monopoly.
6. Centralization of the means of communication and transportation in the hands of the State.
7. Extension of factories and instruments of production owned by the State, the bringing into cultivation of waste lands, and the improvement of soil generally in accordance with a common plan.
8. Equal liability of all to labor. Establishment of industrial armies, especially for agriculture.
9. Combination of agriculture with manufacturing industries, gradual abolition of the distinction between town and country, by a more equable distribution of population over the country.

10. Free education for all children in public schools. Abolition of children's factory labor in its present form. Combination of education with industrial production, etc., etc."

Included as part of the translation are a question and answer section. One such combination is especially informing, restating and expanding on those ten planks listed above:

"QUESTION 18. What will be the course of this revolution?

Answer. Above all, it will establish a democratic constitution, and through this the direct or indirect dominance of the proletariat. ... The main measures, emerging as the necessary result of existing relations, are the following:

(1)   Limitation of Private Property through progressive taxation, heavy inheritance taxes, abolition of inheritance through collateral lines (brothers, nephews, etc.), forced loans, etc.

(2)   Gradual expropriation of landowners, industrialists, railroad magnates and shipowners, partly through competition by state industry, partly directly through compensation in the form of bonds.

(3)   Confiscation of the possessions of all emigrants and rebels against the majority of the people.

(4)   Organization of labor or employment of proletarians on publicly owned land, in factories and workshops, with competition among the workers being abolished and with the factory owners, insofar as they still exist, being obliged to pay the same high wages as those paid by the state.

(5)   An equal obligation on all members of society to work until such time as private property has been completely abolished. Formation of industrial armies, especially for agriculture.

(6)   Centralization of money and credit in the hands of the state through a national bank operating with state capital, and the suppression of all private banks and bankers.

(7)   Expansion of the number of national factories, workshops, railroads, ships; bringing new lands into cultivation and improvement of land already under cultivation – all in proportion to the growth of capital and labor force at the disposal of the nation.

(8)   Education of all children, from the moment they can leave their mothers' care, in national establishments at national cost. Education and production together.

(9)   Construction, on public lands, of great places as communal

dwellings for associated groups of citizens engaged in both industry and agriculture and combining in their way of life the advantages of urban and rural conditions while avoiding the one-sidedness and drawbacks of each.

(10)   Destruction of all unhealthy and jerry-built dwellings in urban districts.

(11)   Equal inheritance rights for children born in and out of wedlock.

(12)   Concentration of all means of transportation in the hands of the nation.

It is impossible, of course, to carry out all these measures at once. …"

Oh Where Can Michigan Be?

The State of Michigan has had four Constitutions. The first one dates back to 1850, before we officially became a State, the second came in 1895, the third in 1908. Four attempts were made to replace the Constitution of 1908 and finally in 1963 it was.

In that rewrite, two entire sections were removed. Both of these sections appeared in all previous versions, with almost no changes made to them during the first 130+ years of our State's history, but suddenly they were dropped.

The two sections removed were: "BOUNDARIES AND SEAT OF GOVERNMENT" and "MILITIA".

BOUNDARIES AND SEAT OF GOVERNMENT:

"BOUNDARIES" was a description of the perimeter of the State of Michigan, or in other words, the "property lines". "BOUNDARIES" was a little bit confusing to read, but if you read it with a map alongside, it's easy enough to follow.

"SEAT OF GOVERNMENT" simply stated that our capital was in Lansing.

In the first two Constitutions, this section was divided into Article I and Article II, in the third they were combined into Article I. In all three of these Constitutions, it was the very first thing (besides the Table of Contents).

Being first makes sense. "BOUNDARIES" are the most basic of facts. When you go to purchase a piece of property, one of the first things you want to know is "where are the property lines?" Once you have *that* information, *then* you raise other questions such as "what are the physical things located on that property", "are there any rules, regulations and/or laws which limits what can be done on/with the property?"

Boundaries are important in many aspects of our lives. Where are the borders Of Wayne County? Of Dearborn? Which voting precinct do you live in? All these answers are based on lines we draw in the sand, then make them *official* and *legal* by writing them down and signing on the dotted line. Why, I remember when I was a kid sitting in the back seat of the car with my older brother. We would draw an imaginary line down the center of the seat and we'd start wailing if the other brother "crossed that line". From the earliest stages of life, until the inevitable grave site, borders, property lines, boundaries play an important role.

So where are Michigan's borders and why were they removed from our State Constitution?

Rob, at the Council of State Governments, an organization in Lexington, Kentucky who studies and compares the governments of all the States, told me that *all* the States have had their BOUNDARIES removed from their Constitutions. "Why would they have done that, Rob? "...probably because they were considered archaic, that in today's day and age we don't need them anymore."

Archaic? Don't need them anymore?

Fred Headen, at The Citizen's Research Council of Michigan, a non-profit group in Detroit and Lansing, examined a document that his organization published at the time of the re-write of Michigan's Constitution. He told me that there's been a *Model State Constitution* circulating for decades, and that his document stated that the *Model* did not contain the BOUNDARIES section, nor the MILITIA section (briefly mentioned above). He also stated that he believed the *Model* probably had much to do with why those sections were dropped.

Who composed and circulated that *Model State Constitution*? The National Civic League out of Denver, Colorado. The information packet the NCL sent me states "The National Civic League (NCL) advocates a new civic agenda... Founded in 1894 by Theodore Roosevelt and other turn-of-the-century progressives...accomplishes its mission through technical assistance, training, publishing, research, and an awards program."

They have a "mission". They do what they do for a reason. Wonder what that reason is? (Note that you'll be hearing more about Theodore Roosevelt, other turn-of-the-century progressives, and the 'techniques' listed above in other info-documents I will be composing...You may start to see a pattern.)

Nearly 50 years ago, the United Nations published a map of the continental United States. It did NOT include the 48 States, but instead it had the country divided into 10 regions. This suggests that from the point of view of "the world", Michigan is meaningless. In fact, according to that map, we live in Region 5, The Great Lakes Region, and our region's capital is Chicago.

So that was 50 years ago. The map probably disappeared because it was unimportant, right? Not hardly.

I stopped at the library and made a photocopy of a page of *The United States Government Manual*, 1994/1995 edition. That map appears below. It does still include the States, but it also clearly shows the 10 regions. Note that we are indeed in region 5 (Roman Numeral V) and there's a big dot near the word Chicago (and no mention of Lansing).

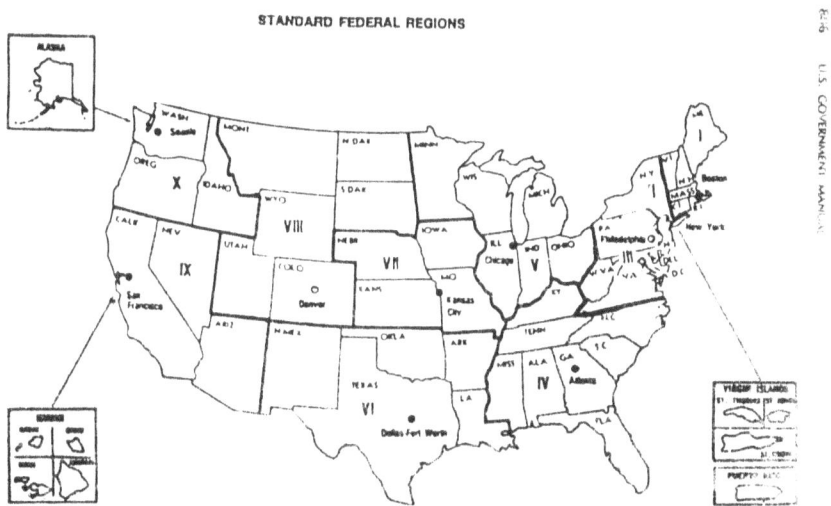

A corresponding description of these regions states: "…and agencies are required to adopt the uniform system when changes are made or new offices established." Clearly, our own Federal Government has adopted the United Nations view of our country, has published it as their own view, and is ordering all U.S. Government agencies to do the same.

Am I some paranoid freak going off on a tangent about the United Nations? Well, if I am, I'm not alone.

Did you know that on March 29, 1994, the State of Oklahoma was the first State to pass legislation which demands that the U.S. Government STOP their involvement with the United Nations. That legislation, HR1047, includes the following excerpts:

"WHEREAS, global government would mean the destruction of our Constitution and corruption of the spirit of the Declaration of Independence, our freedom, and our way of life.

"…Cease engagement in any military activity under the authority of the United Nations or any world body;

"…Cease any support for the establishment of a "new world order" or any form of global government."

Did you know that during the weeks before the Oklahoma City bombing that some of our own State Representatives proposed very similar legislation for the State of Michigan, and that immediately after the Oklahoma bombing that the discussion of that legislation in Lansing was completely dropped?

Did you know that earlier this year, in the City of Sterling Heights, an agenda item titled "To consider the multi-national flag display alternatives" at a City Council meeting provoked such an unexpected overwhelming turnout of citizens, at the meeting, protesting the idea of flying the United Nations flag, that City Council passed a resolution stating: "...resolved that the only national or international flag that will fly over City Hall shall be the United States of America flag, now and in the future."

I'm not alone in my view of the United Nations. If you didn't realize all this was going on, then I'm glad I could fill you in. If you did know, then you must already understand what I am saying...

Our U.S. Constitution, and our country, is based on (50) States, not on the 10 regions defined by the United Nations!

So what about Michigan's borders and its Constitution?

This is most likely not the kind of thing you want to spend your day worrying about. It is, however, the type of thing that our representatives should spend their time worrying about. Our representatives should be doing everything they can to assure that they are keeping our state safe.

Edmund Pendleton, a Virginia judge who helped "sell" the original U.S. Constitution, stated: "Our dearest rights, life, liberty, and property - ...are still in the hands of our state legislature. If they prove too feeble to protect us, we resort to the aid of the general government for security." In other words, if the government of a State is too wimpy then the federal government will step in. The only reason that the U.S. Government gets away with doing many of the things they do is because our State government is too "feeble".

Is your State Government too *feeble*? Is it time that we had real strength and courage in Lansing? Remember that the government, both in Lansing and in Washington, works for you! Lansing should be telling Washington what to do, not the other way around!

Put some real strength and Courage in Lansing!
Please Call!
Please Help!

Note that due to space constraints, I was unable to include in my campaign literature one additional bit of information in connection to the regions defined by the United Nations. It is worth including here:

The regions are defined as I – X (or 1 through 10). Which region do you live in? Take the first digit of your Zip Code. Add one to that first digit and you have your region. Zip Codes range from 0xxxx through 9xxxx while the regions range from 1 through 10. Apparently the easiest way to adapt the regional definitions was to add a one as described above. Indeed, the U.S. Government has gone forward with going along with the United Nations.

Is this numbering system something to worry about? Not necessarily. However, is there something else being planned for us?

Laws Laws Laws

When I want to get a conversation going, and steer it towards "government", I like to ask: "Why do we have a seat belt law?" I'm fascinated by the way folks attempt to justify it. "Because it can save your life" is what most of the answers revolve around. So I continue with: "Then do we need a law to make it illegal to step out of a 20th floor window?" which usually provokes ridicule such as "Don't be stupid."

Frankly, I don't see the difference. I could get killed if I stepped out a 20th floor window. Isn't that the same thing?

I think the idea behind the seat belt law is that government is trying to help protect me. Well, that's very nice. However, there are many things that I do NOT need them to help protect me from, nor do I wish them to spend my money on. I don't need them to demand that I wear my seat belt, charge money so that they can continuously verify that I am indeed wearing my seat belt, then charge me *more* money if they catch me *not* wearing it. Frankly, I'm smart enough to wear it without their "help".

Most folks know that if a fast moving object strikes a stationary object, at least one of the objects may get damaged. Let's do an experiment to prove this point. Moving your hand as swiftly as you possibly can, slap yourself across the face. If you don't see my point immediately, do it again. Eventually, you may be convinced that when a swift moving object strikes a stationary object, at least one of the objects may get damaged.

Government does not need to write laws concerning these things. There are already laws which have them covered. They're called "Laws of Nature". In order to understand the Laws of Nature, a person needs knowledge (not government). I've been wearing my seat belt for decades, because of knowledge. I avoid walking out 20th floor windows, because of knowledge. *Government need not, MUST NOT, waste their time, and my money, writing and enforcing needless laws.* Instead, our citizenry needs to accumulate knowledge.

As a side bar, I wonder how many folks still don't wear their seat belts, preferring to be "criminals" and experience the pangs of anxiety which well up inside them when a police officer is sighted. I wonder if government has really "helped" us, or whether they have simply *created more criminals* and increased the stress level in folks who might otherwise be law-abiding citizens.

In most cases, when a law is written, more of our freedom is stolen from us. More laws usually mean that (if we're going to be law-abiding citizens) there are fewer things that we are "allowed" to do. However, in order to live together in the most peaceful and prosperous society that we can achieve, some laws need to be written. In order to maximize the freedom that we all should cherish, we must keep those laws to a minimum. So how do we decide which laws are necessary?

My freedom ends where your nose begins.

Freedom means that each of us can do what each of us wants to do, in our own pursuit of life, liberty, and property. However, if one person does something that infringes upon another person's freedom, or his life, liberty or property, then we have a problem. As stated above, we write laws so that we can "live together". In order for us to "live together", we cannot infringe on each other's freedom, life, liberty or property. *THAT* is what (most, if not all of) our laws need to be based on, making sure that if one person infringes on the freedom, life, liberty or property of another, that the infringement will stop.

That also means, that if there is no victim, that if no *other* person has been infringed upon, then (most likely) no law should be written. Why not? Because (as stated above) we must also maximize freedom.

In fact, any *law* which infringes on a person's freedom, life, liberty or property, makes *worse* our ability to "live together". The more laws written, the more that *government infringes on our freedoms.*

We have far too many laws which go way beyond this simple rule. Lucky for us, our Founding Fathers foresaw this very thing as being inevitable, thus they supplied us with several tools for ridding ourselves of laws which steal our freedom (without improving our ability to "live together"). One of those tools seems to have been forgotten, one which *each* of us needs to know that *we all can and need to utilize*:

In 1895, the U.S. Supreme Court ruled that it is no longer required to inform the "jury" about this tool, that as a "free" people we could learn about this tool ourselves. What is this tool?

'In 1804, Samuel Chase, Supreme Court Justice and signer of the Declaration of Independence, said,

"The jury has a right to judge both law as well as the facts." '

The above is quoted from the *Juror's Handbook* published by Justice Pro Se of Michigan, PO Box 1809, Dearborn, MI 48121. *When any one of us sits on a jury, WE have the power to declare a law unjust or unconstitutional and thus invalid, not just reach a verdict of guilt or innocence with regards to the defendant!* The handbook quoted above describes this in very clear detail, in a pocket-sized 14 paged pamphlet, ending with:

'**...IF YOU DON'T KNOW YOUR RIGHTS, YOU DON'T HAVE ANY!**' Again, the key is knowledge...

If our government is truly interested in helping to protect us, why aren't they telling us things like this? Why aren't they providing us with knowledge?

Who can write laws? The U.S. Constitution states:

> "Section. 8. The Congress shall have the Power... To make all Laws which shall be necessary and proper for carrying into Execution the foregoing Powers vested by this Constitution in the Government of the United States, or in any Department or Officer thereof."

According to the U.S. Constitution, *only* Congress has the power to write laws. Our government no longer follows this rule.

In *The Making of America*, published in 1986 by the National Center for Constitutional Studies, Washington, D.C., it is stated:

> 'Ever since the Interstate Commerce Commission was developed in 1887, various governmental agencies have been issuing edicts known as "administrative law"... Today more laws are imposed on the American people by these unconstitutional and irregular means than are passed by Congress.'

Our Founding Fathers never envisioned the U.S. President as a "king" who could write his own laws. More from *The Making of America*:

> 'From this point on, each President looked upon executive orders as a tool... President "Teddy" Roosevelt held to the view that he could do anything not specifically prohibited by the Constitution. He missed the Founder's doctrine of enumerated powers, which said he could do NOTHING except that which the Constitution authorized... President Theodore Roosevelt...issued 1,006!'

10th Amendment Resolution.

We don't *only* have the problem of laws being written by folks in government who do not have the power to write them. We *also* have the problem of Congress, who is supposed to have the power, writing laws that go far beyond what the U.S. Constitution allows them to write.

The 10th Amendment states: "The powers not delegated to the United States by the Constitution, nor prohibited by it to the States, are reserved to the States respectively, or to the people."

The governments in many states in our country have finally had enough. After about two years of effort, as of 7/25/95, 20 states have passed legislation which addresses this issue, while many others are still working on it. Some of the legislation is more insistent than others, some discuss "unfunded mandates" while others demand that the U.S. Government stop writing unconstitutional laws.

Michigan is still working on this legislation. In 1994 it was passed in the House of Representatives but "ran out of time" before it passed in the Senate. We have started the process again in 1995. An excerpt from Michigan's legislation:

"Resolved, That we hereby memorialize the federal government, as our agent, to cease and desist, effective immediately, mandates that are beyond the scope of its constitutionally delegated powers..."

Even cities are passing similar legislation. Riverview was the first in our state to do so, and since then several more have done so including neighboring cities such as Wyandotte and Melvindale.

In my eyes, this is only a first step. I believe we will need even stronger offensive action. Note another excerpt from the same proposed Michigan legislation quoted above:

"WHEREAS, The United States Supreme Court has ruled in New York v. United States 112 S. Ct. 2408 (1992), that Congress may not simply commandeer the legislative and regulatory processes of the states,"

Even the U.S. Supreme Court agrees...

(Note that on 7/24/95 I called our current representative in Lansing. I asked Pat in her office how our representative had voted on the 10th Amendment legislation which passed in the House of Representatives late last year. Pat asked her. She said that she didn't recall *how* she had voted on it or *if* she had voted on it.)

You *now* know who is supposed to be writing laws, you know how to eliminate bad laws, you know what kind of laws should exist in a "free" society, and you know that your current government has been ignoring the U.S. Constitution, *the law of the land.*

Use your knowledge to do the right thing!
Please Call!
Please Help!

Note that due to space constraints, I was unable to include in my campaign literature some additional information in connection to a couple of items discussed above. It is worth including here:

The legislature in Michigan promised when they passed the seat belt law that it was never to be a *"primary enforcement"* law, or in other words that no one would ever get pulled over based on whether the police officer noted that a seat belt was being worn, but instead only a *"secondary enforcement"* law, that if a person had been pulled over for *some other infraction* and it was then noticed that the seat belt was not in use, then and only then would a seat belt ticket be issued. Well, you know what's happened. Seat belt wearing is indeed now used as a *"primary enforcement"* law.

The discussion about a juror being able to judge the law as well as the defendant refers to a process that is more commonly known as *"jury nullification"*. You may hear stories about potential jurors being rejected for jury duty simply because they are knowledgeable about the *"jury nullification"* concept. Government prosecutors are not appreciative of jurors who know their rights, and understand the law.

THE DECLARATION OF INDEPENDENCE

Action of Second Continental Congress, July 4, 1776
The unanimous Declaration of the thirteen United States of America

WHEN in the Course of human Events, it becomes necessary for one People to dissolve the Political Bands which have connected them with another, and to assume among the Powers of the Earth, the separate and equal Station to which the Laws of Nature and of Nature's God entitle them, a decent Respect to the Opinions of Mankind requires that they should declare the causes which impel them to the Separation.

WE hold these Truths to be self-evident, that all Men are created equal, that they are endowed by their Creator with certain unalienable Rights, that among these are Life, Liberty, and the Pursuit of Happiness – That to secure these Rights, Governments are instituted among Men, deriving their just Powers from the Consent of the Governed, that whenever any Form of Government becomes destructive of these Ends, it is the Right of the People to alter or to abolish it, and to institute new Government, laying its Foundation on such Principles, and organizing its Powers in such Form, as to them shall seem most likely to effect their Safety and Happiness. Prudence, indeed, will dictate that Governments long established should not be changed for light and transient Causes; and accordingly all Experience hath shewn, that Mankind are more disposed to suffer, while Evils are sufferable, than to right themselves by abolishing the Forms to which they are accustomed. But when a long Train of Abuses and Usurpations, pursuing invariably the same Object, evinces a Design to reduce them under absolute Despotism, it is their Right, it is their Duty, to throw off such Government, and to provide new Guards for their future Security. Such has been the patient Sufferance of these Colonies; and such is now the Necessity which constrains them to alter their former Systems of Government. The History of the present King of Great-Britain is a History of repeated Injuries and Usurpations, all having in direct Object the Establishment of an absolute Tyranny over these States. To prove this, let Facts be submitted to a candid World.

HE has refused his Assent to Laws, the most wholesome and necessary for the public Good.

HE has forbidden his Governors to pass Laws of immediate and pressing Importance, unless suspended in their Operation till his Assent should be obtained; and when so suspended, he has utterly neglected to attend to them.

HE has refused to pass other Laws for the Accommodation of large Districts of People, unless those People would relinquish the Right of Representation in the Legislature, a Right inestimable to them, and formidable to Tyrants only.

HE has called together Legislative Bodies at Places unusual, uncomfortable, and distant from the Depository of their public Records, for the sole Purpose of fatiguing them into Compliance with his Measures.

HE has dissolved Representative Houses repeatedly, for opposing with manly Firmness his Invasions on the Rights of the People.

HE has refused for a long Time, after such Dissolutions, to cause others to be elected; whereby the Legislative Powers, incapable of Annihilation, have returned to the People at large for their exercise; the State remaining in the mean time exposed to all the Dangers of Invasion from without, and Convulsions within.

HE has endeavoured to prevent the Population of these States; for that Purpose obstructing the Laws of Naturalization of Foreigners; refusing to pass others to encourage their Migrations hither, and raising the Conditions of new Appropriations of Lands.

HE has obstructed the Administration of Justice, by refusing his Assent to Laws for establishing Judiciary Powers.

HE has made Judges dependent on his Will alone, for the Tenure of their Offices, and the Amount and Payment of their Salaries.

HE has erected a Multitude of new Offices, and sent hither Swarms of Officers to harass our People, and eat out their

Substance.

HE has kept among us, in Times of Peace, Standing Armies, without the consent of our Legislatures.

HE has affected to render the Military independent of and superior to the Civil Power.

HE has combined with others to subject us to a Jurisdiction foreign to our Constitution, and unacknowledged by our Laws; giving his Assent to their Acts of pretended Legislation:

FOR quartering large Bodies of Armed Troops among us:

FOR protecting them, by mock Trial, from Punishment for any Murders which they should commit on the Inhabitants of these States:

FOR cutting off our Trade with all Parts of the World:

FOR imposing Taxes on us without our Consent:

FOR depriving us, in many Cases, of the Benefits of Trial by Jury:

FOR transporting us beyond Seas to be tried for pretended Offences:

FOR abolishing the free System of English Laws in a neighbouring Province, establishing therein an arbitrary Government, and enlarging its Boundaries, so as to render it at once an Example and fit Instrument for introducing the same absolute Rule into these Colonies:

FOR taking away our Charters, abolishing our most valuable Laws, and altering fundamentally the Forms of our Governments:

FOR suspending our own Legislatures, and declaring themselves invested with Power to legislate for us in all Cases whatsoever.

HE has abdicated Government here, by declaring us out of his Protection and waging War against us.

HE has plundered our Seas, ravaged our Coasts, burnt our Towns, and destroyed the Lives of the People.

HE is, at this Time, transporting large Armies of foreign Mercenaries to compleat the Works of Death, Desolation, and Tyranny, already begun with circumstances of Cruelty and Perfidy, scarcely paralleled in the most barbarous Ages, and totally unworthy the Head of a civilized Nation.

HE has constrained our fellow Citizens taken Captive on the high Seas to bear Arms against their Country, to become the Executioners of their Friends and Brethren, or to fall themselves by their Hands.

HE has excited domestic Insurrections amongst us, and has endeavoured to bring on the Inhabitants of our Frontiers, the merciless Indian Savages, whose known Rule of Warfare, is an undistinguished Destruction, of all Ages, Sexes and Conditions.

IN every stage of these Oppressions we have Petitioned for Redress in the most humble Terms: Our repeated Petitions have been answered only by repeated Injury. A Prince, whose Character is thus marked by every act which may define a Tyrant, is unfit to be the Ruler of a free People.

NOR have we been wanting in Attentions to our British Brethren. We have warned them from Time to Time of Attempts by their Legislature to extend an unwarrantable Jurisdiction over us. We have reminded them of the Circumstances of our Emigration and Settlement here. We have appealed to their native Justice and Magnanimity, and we have conjured them by the Ties of our common Kindred to disavow these Usurpations, which, would inevitably interrupt our Connections and Correspondence. They too have been deaf to the Voice of Justice and of Consanguinity. We must, therefore, acquiesce in the Necessity, which denounces our Separation, and hold them, as we hold the rest of Mankind, Enemies in War, in Peace, Friends.

WE, therefore, the Representatives of the UNITED STATES OF AMERICA, in GENERAL CONGRESS, Assembled, appealing to the Supreme Judge of the World for the Rectitude of our Intentions, do, in the Name, and by Authority of the good People of these Colonies, solemnly Publish and Declare, That these United Colonies are, and of Right ought to be, FREE AND INDEPENDENT STATES; that they are absolved from all Allegiance to the British Crown, and that all political Connection between them and the State of Great-Britain, is and ought to be totally dissolved; and that as FREE AND INDEPENDENT STATES, they have full Power to levy War, conclude Peace, contract Alliances, establish Commerce, and to do all other Acts and Things which INDEPENDENT STATES may of right do. And for the support of this Declaration, with a firm Reliance on the Protection of divine Providence, we mutually pledge to each other our Lives, our Fortunes, and our sacred Honor.

ENDNOTES

[1] *The Wall Street Journal,* May 9, 1995

[2] From *The Report From Iron Mountain*, page viii

[3] From *The Report From Iron Mountain*, page ix

[4] From *The Report From Iron Mountain*, page xxii

[5] From *The Report From Iron Mountain*, page 44

[6] From *The Report From Iron Mountain*, page 67

[7] From *The Report From Iron Mountain*, page x

[8] From *The Report From Iron Mountain*, page 89

[9] From *The Report From Iron Mountain*, pages xi and xii

[10] From *The Tipping Point*, page 177

[11] From *The Tipping Point*, page 179

[12] From *The Tipping Point*, page 179-180

[13] From *The Tipping Point*, pages 180-181

[14] From *The Tipping Point*, pages 183-185

[15] From *The Making of America,* 1986, page 678

[16] From *The Making of America*, 1986, page 265

[17] From *The Making of America*, 1986, page 657

[18] From www.merrycoz.org article entitled *The American Spelling Book,* by Noah Webster (1800?)

[19] *Juror's Handbook*, 1995, page 5

[20] From the dust jacket of the 60th Anniversary Edition of *We The Living*

[21] Changed by section 2 of the Fourteenth Amendment

[22] Changed by the Seventeenth Amendment

[23] Changed by the Seventeenth Amendment

[24] Changed by section 2 of the Twentieth Amendment

[25] See Sixteenth Amendment

[26] Changed by the Twelfth Amendment

[27] Changed by the Twenty-Fifth Amendment

[28] Changed by the Eleventh Amendment

[29] Changed by the Eleventh Amendment

[30] Changed by the Thirteenth Amendment

[31] The first ten Amendments (Bill of Rights) were ratified effective December 15, 1791.

[32] The Eleventh Amendment was ratified February 7, 1795.

[33] The Twelfth Amendment was ratified June 15, 1804.

[34] Superseded by section 3 of the Twentieth Amendment

[35] The Thirteenth Amendment was ratified December 6, 1865.

[36] The Fourteenth Amendment was ratified July 9, 1868.

[37] The Fifteenth Amendment was ratified February 3, 1870.

[38] The Sixteenth Amendment was ratified February 3, 1913.

[39] The Seventeenth Amendment was ratified April 8, 1913.

[40] The Eighteenth Amendment was ratified January 16, 1919. It was repealed by the Twenty-First Amendment, December 5, 1933.

[41] The Nineteenth Amendment was ratified August 18, 1920.

[42] The Twentieth Amendment was ratified January 23, 1933.

[43] The Twenty-First Amendment was ratified December 5, 1933.

[44] The Twenty-Second Amendment was ratified February 17, 1951.

[45] The Twenty-Third Amendment was ratified March 29, 1961.

[46] The Twenty-Fourth Amendment was ratified January 23, 1964.

[47] The Tweny-Fifth Amendment was ratified February 10, 1967.

[48] The Twenty-Sixth Amendment was ratified July 1, 1971.

[49] Congress submitted the text of the Twenty-Seventh Amendment to the States as part of the proposed Bill of Rights on September 25, 1789. The Amendment was not ratified together with the first ten Amendments, which became effective on December 15, 1971. The Twenty-Seventh Amendment was ratified on May 7, 1992, by the vote of Michigan.